MW01277384

CONTEMPORARY HOTEL DESIGN

JOACHIM FISCHER

CONTEMPORARY HOTEL DESIGN

DOM
publishers

DEUTSCH

VORWORT

HOTELS SIND ORTE, die dem Gast in wenigen Stunden oder Tagen andere Erlebnisse bieten können als die vom Alltag her bekannten Situationen. Die Hülle Hotel muss die emotionalen Welten des modernen Lebensstils nicht nur zulassen, sondern mit all ihren Details aufnehmen und verfeinern. Das vorliegende Buch über Design und Architektur von Hotels ist in dieser Hinsicht eine Publikation der besonderen Art. Einerseits berücksichtigt es nur Hotels, die von Ende 2006 bis Ende 2007 eröffnet wurden. Anderseits ist es aufwendig und liebevoll illustriert – mit Bildern, die wesentlich durch die Materialien, das Design und das Ambiente bestimmt sind.

Das Geschäft mit Hotels boomt. Nicht nur mehr vereinzelte, innovative Hoteliers, sondern inzwischen auch internationale Hotelketten und deren Investoren entdecken Architektur und Design als zentralen Bestandteil für die Akzeptanz und damit den Erfolg von Hotelprojekten. Mit der steigenden Nachfrage wächst der Markt für exklusive wie individuelle Produkte in neue Sphären. Die Möglichkeiten werden immer vielfältiger: vom kleinen Hotel in der Toskana über das ultimative hippe Stadthotel bis hin zur Privatlodge mit persönlichem Service – alles wird geboten.

Nun hat man nicht nur die Qual der Wahl zwischen den verschiedenen Orten weltweit, sondern man kann sich auch noch zwischen traditionellen, klassischen, modernen und trendigen Unterkünften entscheiden. Die Gegensätze könnten größer nicht sein: dicke Teppiche, die jeden Schall schlucken,

ENGLISH

EDITORIAL

HOTELS ARE PLACES in which, during only a few hours or days, the guest can enjoy experiences different to those with which he is familiar in everyday life. The shell of a hotel must not only let in the emotional worlds of the modern lifestyle, but also absorb and refine them in all their detail. In this regard, the present book on design and architecture in hotels is a very special publication. On the one hand, it explores only those hotels which were opened between the end of 2006 and the end of 2007 while, on the other, the book is lovingly and elaborately enhanced with illustrations which have largely been suggested by the materials, design and ambience.

The hotel business is booming. It is not only individual, innovative hoteliers but also international hotel chains and their investors who are discovering architecture and design as central elements for the success acceptance and subsequent success of hotel projects. With increasing demand, the market for exclusive and individual products is growing to ever greater heights. The choice is becoming increasingly varied: from a small hotel in Tuscany or the ultimate hip city hotel to the private lodge with personal service – anything is possible.

Now one not only has the torment of choosing between various places throughout the world, but one also has to decide on whether accommodation should be traditional, classic, modern or hip. The contrasts couldn't be greater: thick carpets that swallow every

DEUTSCH

Pop-Art und Dance-Club in ein und demselben Gebäude. Schlägt das Herz eher für familiäre Vertrautheit oder doch für wohltuende Anonymität? Entspannt man sich besser in gemütlicher Runde oder im exklusiven Ski-Resort?

Das Thema Hoteldesign ist hoch sensibel und zeigt sich heutzutage als kenntnisreiche Leidenschaft: Die Kunden sehnen sich nach dem Besonderen und Individuellen – dem Emotionalen und dem Authentischen. Durch die weltweite Vernetzung von Hotels, Architekten, Designern, Anlässen und Orten entstehen Produkte, die ein einzigartiges, emotionalisierendes Erlebnis auf höchstem Niveau ermöglichen. Über das eigentliche Thema Hotel hinaus wird somit ein attraktiver Mehrwert geboten, der für Geld nicht ohne Weiteres käuflich ist.

Trotz Globalisierung und eines weltweiten stilistischen Geschmacks: In den hier präsentierten Beispielen sind die unterschiedlichen, oftmals sehr persönlich geprägten Gestaltungsansätze auffallend. Selbstverständlich ist die vorgestellte Auswahl der neu eröffneten Hotels nicht komplett; aus Platzgründen konnten nicht alle aufgenommen werden und einzelne Häuser waren – in der Tat – zu »alt«. Die folgenden Seiten sollen jedoch dazu verführen, sich bei der Wahl des Reiseziels, eines Hotels bewusst die für den Einzelnen individuell passende Atmosphäre zu wählen.

Dies ist eine Sammlung der besten Designkonzepte aus aller Welt – ein Feuerwerk innovativer Ideen, das die Trends zu einem faszinierenden Kompendium zusammenführt.

ENGLISH

sound or pop art and dance club in the same building. Would one prefer familiar surroundings or restful anonymity? Can one relax better in a cosy group or at an exclusive ski resort?

The subject of hotel design is highly emotive and is discussed today with a well-informed passion. Guests yearn for something special and individual – the emotional and authentic. Thanks to the global networking of hotels, architects, designers, events and places, products are being created which achieve the highest peaks of unique, emotionalising experience. Thus beyond the structure of the hotel itself, an attractive added value is offered, which cannot simply be had for money.

Despite globalisation and a universal taste with regard to style, the varying, often highly personalised designs of the examples presented here are quite striking. Naturally, for reasons of space, the selection of newly opened hotels is not comprehensive and, indeed, some of the hotels were in fact too »old«. It is hoped, however, that this book will persuade readers to consciously choose a hotel with the atmosphere that suits them.

This is a collection of the best design concepts from all over the world. It is a firework display of innovative ideas, which collects individual trends into a single, fascinating compendium.

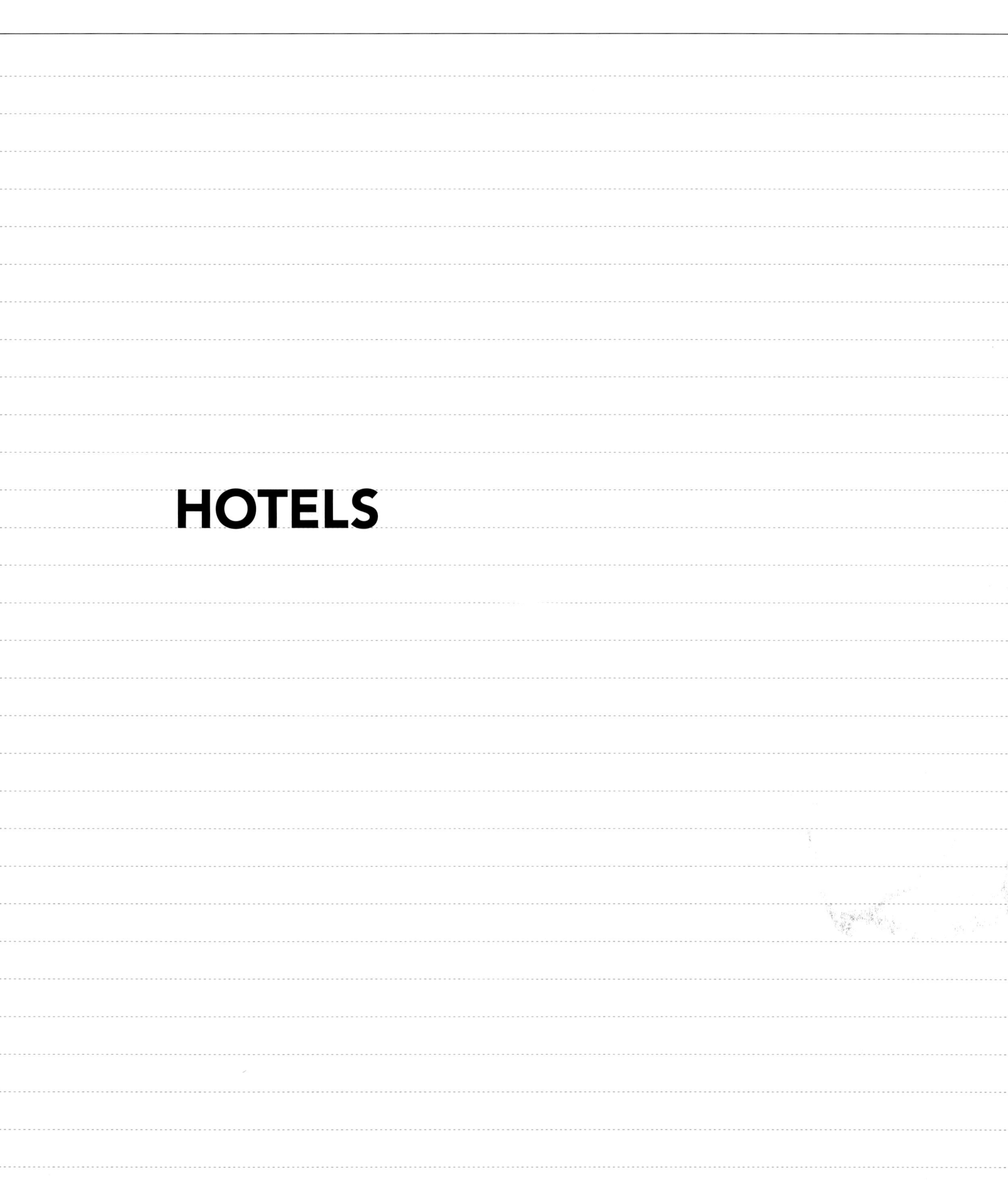

HOTELS

DEUTSCH

ENGLISH

ADAM & EVE HOTEL

Antalya, Turkey

IM ADAM & EVE ZU WOHNEN, das bedeutet viel mehr als nur fernab der Heimat zu übernachten. Weit weg von Alltagsstress und Sorgen können die Gäste das genießen, wovon andere nur träumen. Denn das Adam & Eve gleicht keinem anderen Hotel – es hat seinen ganz individuellen Reiz. Die pure, weiße Einrichtung bietet die perfekte, neutrale Fläche für überraschende Lichteffekte. Und es ist auch ein Hotel der Superlative: Der Pool hat doppelte Olympialänge und die Bar ist mit ihren 88 Metern sicher eine der längsten der Welt.

Im Adam & Eve sind auch die Zimmer postmoderne Kunstwerke. Vom weichen, weißen Fußboden bis hin zu den raumhohen Spiegelwänden, in denen sich Licht und Wasser millionenfach brechen und spiegeln – das Erlebnis ist ein visuell provokatives Statement zum Design. Sinnlichkeit durch Purismus: Das Zimmer selbst verführt mit einem luxuriösen Whirlpool für zwei.

STAYING AT THE ADAM & EVE means much more than just spending a night somewhere a long way from home. Far removed from daily stress and worries, guests enjoy what others can only dream about – because the Adam & Eve is like no other hotel. It has its own very special charm. The pure, white furnishings offer the perfect, natural surface for surprising light effects. And it's also a hotel of superlatives: the pool is double Olympic length and, at almost 289 feet, the bar must surely be one of the longest in the world.

At the Adam & Eve, the rooms are also post-modern works of art. From the soft, white floors to the room height mirrors in which light and water are broken into a million splitters and reflected, the experience is a visually provocative design statement. Sensuality through purism: the room itself seduces with a luxurious whirlpool for two.

Address
Adam & Eve Hotel
Iskele Mevkii
Antalya, Turkey

Website
www.adamevehotels.com

Der Pool – doppeltes Olympiamaß. Ein Paradies für Sonnenanbeter. Von ihrer Unterwasserliege aus blicken sie über das Mittelmeer … // The pool – double Olympic length. A paradise for sun worshippers. From your underwater lounger you look across the Mediterranean …

The beat goes on im Adam & Eve ... Ob in der stylischen Bluetooth Bar im verspiegelten Atrium oder in der schon jetzt legendären Diskothek Lab, wo Musik und Tanz bis zum Morgengrauen weitergehen: Hier ist für jeden etwas dabei. //
The beat goes on in the Adam & Eve ... whether it's in the stylish Bluetooth Bar in the mirrored atrium or in the Adam & Eve's already legendary disco Lab where music and dancing go on 'til dawn. There's something for everybody here.

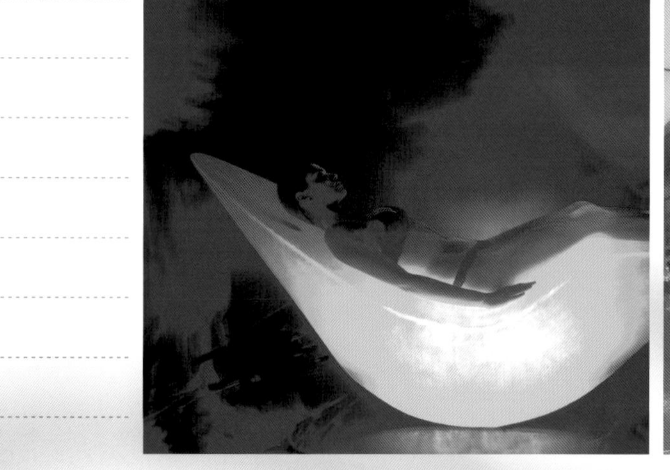

Die Zimmer können je nach persönlicher Stimmung in verschiedenfarbiges Licht getaucht werden: beruhigendes Blau, strahlendes Gelb oder meditatives Violett. // Depending on the guest's mood, the rooms can be illuminated with different coloured light: relaxing blue, glowing yellow or meditative violet.

5.000 Quadratmeter misst der Spa-Bereich des Hotels: Verschiedene Pools und Bäder, einige davon speziell für intime Stunden zu zweit, Saunen und Solarien sind der Entspannung und dem Wohlbefinden gewidmet. // The hotel's spa area takes up almost 54,000 square feet and contains various pools and baths, some of which are specially designed for intimate moments for two, saunas and solariums, all dedicated to relaxation and wellbeing.

DEUTSCH

ENGLISH

HOTEL ANDAZ

London, United Kingdom

IM LONDONER EAST END, nur zehn Gehminuten vom Tower und der Themse entfernt, befindet sich dieses elegante, komfortable Hotel. Das Gebäude wurde bereits 1884 erbaut, im Inneren jedoch findet sich der Gast im 21. Jahrhundert wieder. Der besondere und persönliche Service steht hier im Vordergrund und hat ein innovatives Hotelkonzept hervorgebracht: Die Rezeption und eine traditionelle Lobby fehlen, stattdessen steht den Gästen ein persönlicher Gastgeber (der so genannte ANDAZ Host) zur Verfügung. Der Angestellte erledigt mithilfe eines mobilen Kleincomputers den Check-in.
Design und die Ausstattung sind exklusiv und außergewöhnlich. Die Lobby, die eher einem Wohnzimmer gleicht, empfängt den Gast in gedeckten, dunklen Grautönen. Und auch die vier Restaurants, drei Bars, 14 Veranstaltungsräume und 267 Gästezimmer wurden individuell gestaltet, um das ultimative, moderne Hotelerlebnis möglich zu machen.

THIS ELEGANT and comfortable hotel is located in London's East End, only ten minutes' walk from the Tower of London and the Thames. The building was erected in 1884 but the interior is very definitely 21st century. Special, personal service is in the foreground here and has produced an innovative hotel concept. The reception and traditional lobby are absent. Instead guests have a personal ANDAZ Host who takes care of check-in with a hand held computer. Design and furnishing are exclusive and unusual. The lobby, which is more like a living room, welcomes the guest in muted, dark grey tones. The four restaurants, three bars, 14 event rooms and 267 bedrooms were also designed to create the ultimate, modern hotel experience.

Address
Hotel ANDAZ
40 Liverpool Street
London, UK

Website
london.liverpoolstreet.andaz.com

Die Zimmer wurden mit jeder Art von Annehmlichkeiten ausgestattet. Erholung und Komfort stehen hier an oberster Stelle. Ein luxuriöses Bett, ein großzügiges Badezimmer und ein Arbeitsplatz mit modernster Technik offerieren dem Gast ein unvergessliches Erlebnis. // The rooms are equipped with all modern conveniences. Relaxation and comfort are top priorities. A luxurious bed, a generously-sized bathroom and a work area with the latest technology combine to provide the ultimate, modern hotel experience.

DEUTSCH

ENGLISH

AIRPORT HOTEL

Stuttgart, Germany

IN UNMITTELBARER NÄHE zum Flughafen und zur neuen Landesmesse befindet sich das neueste Hotel der Mövenpick-Kette. Es ist der ideale Ort für einen Zwischenstopp oder für Business-Reisende, die einen angenehmen Platz für effiziente Meetings benötigen. Das moderne, komfortable Viersternehotel beherbergt 326 Zimmer inklusive zwölf Junior-Suiten und zwei Suiten à 71 Quadratmeter. Sie alle verfügen, dank großflächiger Fenster, über viel Tageslicht. Der außergewöhnliche Business-Look wird gepaart mit frischen Farben und wohnlichen Accessoires. Alle Zimmer bieten die Annehmlichkeiten eines Viersterne-Superior-Hotels. Luxuriöse Materialien, ein dezentes Farbkonzept und der einzigartige Umgang mit Licht im gesamten Hotel tragen die Handschrift des berühmten Mailänder Architekten Matteo Thun.

THE LATEST HOTEL in the Mövenpick chain is located immediately adjacent to the airport and the new »Landesmesse« exhibition centre. It is the ideal spot for a stopover or for business travellers who need a pleasant place for efficient meetings. This modern and comfortable four star hotel comprises 326 rooms including twelve Junior Suites and two suites measuring 764 square feet. Thanks to large windows, they all have plenty of daylight. The unusual business look is coupled with fresh colours and homely accessories. All of the rooms offer the usual amenities of a four star superior hotel. Luxurious materials, a subtle colour concept and the unique treatment of light throughout the hotel all bear the signature of the famous Milan architect, Matteo Thun.

Address
Airport Hotel
Flughafenstrasse 50
Stuttgart, Germany

Website
www.moevenpick-hotels.com

Das Restaurant Trollinger mit 174 Sitzplätzen, offenem Kamin und privatem Essbereich bietet neben internationalen Gerichten eine Vielzahl an regionalen Spezialitäten. // The Trollinger Restaurant which seats 174 people, has an open fireplace and a private dining area, and offers a wide variety of regional specialities as well as international dishes.

Von außen besticht das Hotel durch seine moderne Glasarchitektur mit den auffälligen Farbfeldern in verschiedenen Rottönen. // From outside too, the hotel is pleasing with modern glass architecture and striking blocks of red in different shades.

Die Bäder bieten eine Symbiose aus schwarzen Oberflächenmaterialien wie Fliesen, Mosaik, Ornamenttapete und Glas. Zahlreiche qualitativ sehr hochwertig ausgeführte Details wie zum Beispiel das große Fensterelement vom Bad zum Wohnbereich bieten ein exklusives Ambiente. // The bathrooms offer a symbiosis of black surface materials such as tiles, mosaics, decorative wallpaper and glass. There are numerous high quality details such as the large window element between bathroom and living area, which create an exclusive ambience.

SOUNDS
FROM
AVALON
ALL SONGS WRITTEN
AND PRODUCED BY
ERIK TÖRNBLOM
RECORDED AT
TUFF STUDIOS GOTHENBURG
ALL RIGHTS RESERVED
HEART ATTACK MUSIC AB
NOT FOR SALE
MINIBAR
PLEASE
& AVALON MINISHOP
member of
design hotels

DEUTSCH

ENGLISH

AVALON HOTEL

Gothenburg, Sweden

BESUCHER der schwedischen Küstenstadt Göteborg erwartet im Avalon ein einzigartiges Ambiente. In den 101 Hotelzimmern mit 202 Betten wird besonderer Wert auf das harmonische Zusammenspiel von Möblierung, Licht, Düften und Klängen nach den Regeln des Feng-Shui gelegt. Designklassiker von Arne Jacobsen und Farbakzente in gedecktem Blau und Grün geben den Räumen eine elegante Note. Wiederkehrendes Thema ist die Orchidee – als Symbol für Schönheit und Harmonie schmückt die Königin der Blumen jedes einzelne Zimmer des Avalon. Auch die ausgezeichnete Restaurantküche ist einen Besuch wert: Moderne schwedische Kreationen mit Fisch und Meeresfrüchten, aber auch mit exotischen Einflüssen kommen hier auf den Teller. Das Hotel bietet seinen Gästen im Parterre zudem ein Café und eine elf Meter lange Bar. Der Weinkeller des Avalon hält darüber hinaus eine exzellente Auswahl an Weinen mit Schwerpunkt Bordeaux bereit.

VISITORS to the Swedish coastal town of Gothenburg can enjoy the incomparable ambience of the Avalon Hotel. The 101 rooms, with their 202 beds, place particular value on the harmonious interplay of furnishings, light, aromas and sounds, based on the principles of Feng Shui. Design classics from Arne Jacobsen and highlights of colour in muted blue and green lend the rooms a note of elegance. A repeated theme is the orchid – as a symbol of beauty and harmony this queen of flowers ornaments every single room at the Avalon. The hotels's excellent restaurant is also worth a visit. The menu boasts modern Swedish creations with fish and seafood, as well as more exotic fare. On the ground floor, the hotel also has a café and a 36 feet bar. In addition, the Avalon's cellar offers an excellent choice of wines with the emphasis on Bordeaux.

Address
Avalon Hotel
Kungstorget 9
Gothenburg, Sweden

Website
www.avalonhotel.se

Sämtliche Speisekarten und Broschüren sind einheitlich gestaltet. // All menus and brochures have a standard design.

DEUTSCH

ENGLISH

ALTSTADT VIENNA

Vienna, Austria

IN EINEM GEBÄUDE aus der Gründerzeit, im 7. Wiener Bezirk, befindet sich das Altstadt Vienna, dessen acht neue Zimmer und eine Suite von dem italienischen Architekten Matteo Thun gestaltet wurden.

Beim Betreten dieser Räume wird der Gast in das Wien der Jahrhundertwende und in die Welt der berühmtesten Dirne der Stadt, Josefine Mutzenbacher, entführt: Unmittelbar fällt der Blick auf ein großformatiges Bild an der Wand, das jeweils eine Aktstudie aus der Zeit zwischen 1900 und 1950 darstellt.

In allen acht Zimmern dominieren gedämpfte Farben, Parkett aus gebeizter Eiche und Tapeten aus dunklem Damast. Veredelt wird diese dunkle Schwere mit roten Samtmöbeln. Die mondäne Suite ist das so genannte Herrenzimmer. Im Unterschied zu den anderen Räumen ist die Tapete hier gestreift, Sofa und Sessel sind in braunem Leder gepolstert, das Bett besitzt ein dunkles, majestätisches Kopfteil, der Teppich ist cognacfarben. Auffallend ist das offene Badezimmer, mit einer auf einem Podest frei stehenden Badewanne nebst Waschbecken und Spiegel. Baden wird hier auf besondere Art zelebriert, der eigene Körper zur Schau gestellt, ein Ritual der Verführung inszeniert.

SITUATED IN VIENNA'S 7TH DISTRICT, in a building dating back to the Wilhelmine era, the Altstadt Vienna now has eight new rooms and a suite designed by the Italian architect, Matteo Thun.

On entering these rooms, the guest is whisked back to the Vienna of the 1900s and the world of the city's most famous courtesan, Josefine Mutzenbacher: one's eye is immediately caught by the large painting on the wall, depicting a nude study from the period between 1900 and 1950.

Dark colours, pickled oak parquet and dark damask wallpaper dominate in all rooms. This voluptuous darkness is refined with furniture upholstered in red velvet. The hotel's sophisticated suite is known as the Gentleman's Room. Unlike the other rooms, here the wallpaper is striped, sofa and armchairs are upholstered in brown leather, the bed has a dark, majestic headboard and the carpet is cognac coloured. Another striking feature is the open bathroom, in which a freestanding bathtub is set on a dais, beside the washbasin and mirror. Here, bathing is celebrated in its own special way, one's own body is put on display, a ritual of seduction enacted.

Address
Altstadt Vienna
Kirchengasse 41
Vienna, Austria

Website
www.altstadt.at

Jedes der Zimmer hat seinen eigenen Namen, der in den dunkelgrauen, handgefertigten Teppich eingewebt ist. // Each of the rooms has its own name which is woven into the dark grey, handmade carpet.

Die Wände des Badezimmers sind mit Mosaiksteinen komplett in Schwarz gestaltet, einzeln eingefügte Swarovski-Steine setzen Lichtpunkte, der Boden ist aus schwarzem, spiegelndem Marmor. Der dunkle Hintergrund steht in elegantem Kontrast zu den Wasserhähnen in verchromtem Messing und dem kühlen Weiß der Waschbecken und erzeugt eine luxuriöse Atmosphäre. // The walls of the bathroom are completely covered in black mosaic tiles, with individually placed Swarovski stones creating points of light. The floor is made of black, reflective marble. The dark background provides an elegant contrast to the taps in chrome-plated brass and the cool white of the washbasin, creating a luxurious atmosphere.

DEUTSCH

ENGLISH

BLUE PALACE RESORT & SPA

Crete, Greece

DAS BLUE PALACE RESORT & SPA ist das neueste Luxushotel auf der griechischen Mittelmeerinsel Kreta. Ein Resort von außergewöhnlicher Qualität und Eleganz, errichtet in der mythischen Umgebung der vorgelagerten Insel Spinalonga mit ihrer venezianischen Festung aus dem 16. Jahrhundert. Die Anlage ist die ideale Basis für erholsame Ferien, Erkundungen zu den zahlreichen archäologischen Stätten und kulinarische Enddeckungen oder Wanderungen durch die atemberaubenden Landschaften Kretas.

Das Design des Hotels und seiner Gärten wurde im Einklang mit der Natur gestaltet. Die Anlage entfaltet sich in kleinen Einheiten von Bungalows, die sich harmonisch in die ruhige Umgebung einfügen. Errichtet an einem Hang, führt das Resort hinunter zum hoteleigenen Strand. Der Panorama-Lift ermöglicht den einfachen Zugang von allen Ebenen des Hotels. Die 251 Zimmer und Suiten wurden großzügig und geräumig angelegt. Hochwertige Materialien und das harmonische Zusammenspiel exklusiver Möbel mit inseltypischen Elementen bieten ein luxuriöses und elegantes Ambiente zum Entspannen und Erholen.

THE BLUE PALACE RESORT & SPA is the latest luxury hotel on the Greek Mediterranean island of Crete. A resort of extraordinary quality and style, set in the mythical surroundings of the offshore island of Spinalonga with its 16th century Venetian fortress. The resort is an ideal base for relaxing holidays, exploring the numerous archaeological sites, culinary discoveries or rambling through Crete's breathtaking scenery.

The hotel and its gardens were designed to harmonise with the landscape. The resort is made up of small units of bungalows which fit seamlessly into the tranquil surroundings. Built on a slope, the resort goes down to its own beach. The panorama lift provides easy access to all levels of the hotel. The 251 rooms and suites are generously sized and spacious. Opulent materials and the harmonious interplay of exclusive furniture with typical Cretan elements offer a luxurious ambience for relaxation and unwinding.

Address
Blue Palace Resort & Spa
Plaka, Elounda
Crete, Greece

Website
www.bluepalace.gr

Pools mit Meer- oder Süßwasser, beheizbar oder mit Unterwassermusik und private Pools, die mit dem Meer eins zu werden scheinen – hier bleiben keine Wünsche offen. // Saltwater and freshwater pools, heated or with underwater music, private pools which seem to become one with the sea – here, no wish is left unfulfilled.

DEUTSCH

ENGLISH

CASA COLOMBO

Colombo, Sri Lanka

DIE GELUNGENE RESTAURIERUNG eines 200 Jahre alten maurischen Herrenhauses und die Gestaltung der Innenräume mit einer Mischung aus zeitgemäßem Design und traditionellen asiatischen Elementen machen die Casa Colombo zu einem Anziehungspunkt weit gereister Architektur- und Designfreunde. Einst gebaut von einer der wohlhabendsten indischen Kaufmannsfamilien der Insel, besticht das Gebäude durch seine aufwendige Ausstattung mit italienischen und indischen Mosaikböden, steinernen Arkaden, reich verzierten Decken und den maurischen Balkonen.

Die Raumaufteilung des Hauses wurde beibehalten und so hat jede der zwölf Suiten ihren speziellen Grundriss. Unterstrichen wird die Einzigartigkeit der Zimmer dadurch, dass jedes von ihnen eine eigene Farbpalette und somit einen ganz individuellen Charakter erhalten hat.

THE SUCCESSFUL RESTORATION of a 200 year old Moorish mansion and the finishing of the interior rooms using a mix of contemporary design and traditional Asian elements has made the Casa Colombo into a huge draw for lovers of architecture and design from far and wide. Once erected by one of the wealthiest Indian trading families in the island, the building is most pleasing thanks to its detailed decoration with Italian and Indian mosaic floors, stone arcades, richly ornamented ceilings and its Moorish balconies.

The original division of the rooms has been preserved so that each of the twelve suites has its own individual floor plan. The unique quality of the rooms is emphasised by the fact that each is decorated in different colours, so that each one retains its particular character.

Address
Casa Colombo
231 Galle Road
Colombo, Sri Lanka

Website
www.casacolombo.com

Der Pink Pool lädt zum Relaxen ein. Acht gläserne Sonnenliegen und drei großzügige Kanapees sind ausschließlich für Hotelgäste reserviert. // The Pink Pool invites the guest to relax. Eight glass sun loungers and three broad canopies are reserved for the exclusive use of the hotel guests.

Warme Farben, Akzente in Gold und indirektes Licht unterstreichen die Eleganz der Suiten. //
The elegance of the suites is underlined with warm colours, gold highlights and indirect lighting.

Im T Republic werden Ceylon-Tees aus verschiedensten Regionen Sri Lankas angeboten und auf traditionelle Weise serviert. // At the T Republic a selection of Ceylon teas from plantations throughout Sri Lanka are served in the traditional style.

Die Große Halle des Herrenhauses wurde umgebaut zu einem stylischen Restaurant mit goldverzierten Decken, einem riesigen antiken Ventilator, zarten Glastischen und einem Fresko meditierender Mönche. // The Grand Hall of the mansion has been converted into a stylish restaurant with gold ornamented ceiling, an enormous, antique fan, delicate glass tables and a fresco of meditating monks.

DEUTSCH

ENGLISH

CERÊS AM MEER

Baltic Resort of Binz, Germany

DAS THEMA WASSER wird facettenreich im gesamten Hotel zelebriert: vom Spa über die Zimmer bis hin zur Speisekarte. Die Architektur hält sich mit ihrer klaren Formensprache zurück, reduziert sich auf ein Minimum an Elementen und fordert den Gast dazu auf, sich auf das Wesentliche zu beschränken. Ruhe, Balance, Großzügigkeit und Weite spiegeln sich in der Gestaltung des Hotels wider. Diskrete Materialien und eine zurückhaltende Farbkomposition aus Weiß, Grau und Schwarz mit dezenten Akzenten in Silber und Platin lassen das Interieur elegant und luxuriös erstrahlen. Jedes der 42 Zimmer, gegliedert in vier Kategorien, und jede der acht Suiten verfügt über große französische Fenster, einen Balkon oder eine Terrasse sowie geräumige Badezimmer. Das Highlight ist jedoch die Kuppelsuite. Von hier hat der Gast einen atemberaubenden Panoramablick über die Ostsee.

THE THEME OF WATER is celebrated in all its facets throughout the hotel: from the spa and rooms to the menu. With its clean lines, the architecture is restrained, reduced to its elemental minimum, encouraging the guest to focus on the essential. Calm, balance, spaciousness and breadth are reflected in the hotel's design. Muted materials and a subdued colour scheme in white, grey and black with subtle silver and platinum highlights give the interior an elegant and luxurious glow. Each of the 42 rooms, divided into four categories, as well as the eight suites have large French windows, a balcony or terrace and spacious bathrooms. The highlight, however, is the Dome Suite, from where the guest has a breathtaking panorama view of the Baltic.

Address
Cerês am Meer
Strandpromenade 24
Baltic Resort of Binz,
Rügen, Germany

Website
www.ceres-hotel.de

Die regionale Küche des NEGRO spielt mit feinen Aromen und bewegt sich auf internationalem Niveau. Restaurant und Cocktailbar gehen als räumliche Einheit ineinander über; sie grenzen an die Seeterrassen mit Meereskulisse. Und die Lounge lädt mit Blick in den Garten zum Verweilen ein. // The NEGRO's regional cuisine plays with fine flavours and is of international standard. Restaurant and cocktail bar merge with one another as a single space and are adjacent to terraces with sea view. The lounge too, with its view of the garden, is also an ideal place to spend some time.

Im SENSO SPA findet sich die Kernkompetenz des Hauses mit dem Thema Wasser – als Ursprung von allem. Hier werden tiefe, natürliche Empfindungen und Emotionen durch unterschiedliche Wahrnehmungen des Wassers freigesetzt. Dies führt zu unmittelbarem Wohlbefinden und innerer Balance. // At the root of it all, the hotel's core expertise in the subject of water is revealed in the SENSO SPA. Here, deep natural feelings and emotions are released through different perceptions of water, leading to an immediate sensation of wellbeing and inner balance.

THE
CHARLES
HOTEL

DEUTSCH

ENGLISH

THE CHARLES HOTEL

Munich, Germany

DIESES NEUE HOTEL steht im Herzen Münchens, direkt am Alten Botanischen Garten und in der Nähe des Königsplatzes. Alle berühmten Sehenswürdigkeiten der Stadt sind zu Fuß zu erreichen oder liegen nur wenige Autominuten vom Hotel entfernt. Somit ist es idealer Ausgangspunkt zur Erkundung von Museen und der Innenstadt mit den zahlreichen Einkaufsmöglichkeiten in der Fußgängerzone, der Maximilianstraße oder der Residenzstraße. Trotz der zentralen Lage ist das achtgeschossige Hotel eine Oase der Ruhe und bietet sowohl für Geschäftsreisende als auch für Urlauber die ideale Mischung.

Die Inneneinrichtung vermittelt Wohlbehagen auf höchstem Niveau. Warme Farben sowie stilvolles Mobiliar und mit Liebe ausgewählte Wohnaccessoires geben dem Hotel einen besonderen Charme. Ab der sechsten Etage liegen dem Gast sogar die Bayerischen Alpen sowie sämtliche Sehenswürdigkeiten Münchens zu Füßen.

THIS NEW HOTEL is situated in the heart of Munich, directly adjacent to the Old Botanical Gardens and close to Königsplatz. All of Munich's famous sights can easily be reached on foot or are only a few minutes' drive from the hotel. As such, it is the ideal base for exploring both the museums and the city with its numerous shopping options in the pedestrian zone, Maximilianstrasse or Residenzstrasse. Despite its central location, this eight-storey hotel is an oasis of tranquillity and provides the ideal mix for both business travellers or holidaymakers.

The interior design creates an impression of absolute comfort. Warm colours and stylish furnishings, together with lovingly selected accessories give the hotel its particular charm. From the 6th floor upwards, guests also have the Bavarian Alps and all of Munich's sights at their feet.

Address
The Charles Hotel
Sophienstrasse 28
Munich, Germany

Website
www.charleshotel.de

Das südländische Flair ist in diesem Hotel nicht nur im Design zu erkennen, auch das hoteleigene Restaurant Davvero mit separatem Private Dining Room und Sonnenterrasse bietet original italienische Köstlichkeiten an. //
Mediterranean flair is visible not only in the hotel's design, but also in its restaurant Davvero, with its separate Private Dining Room and sun terrace, offering delicious authentic Italian cuisine.

DEUTSCH

ENGLISH

THE CHEDI MILAN

Milan, Italy

IN DESIGNERKREISEN ist Indonesien bekannt für seine sinnlichen Bauwerke und seine ausgefallenen Textilien, Italien dagegen für sein revolutionäres Industriedesign und seine ausgeprägten skulpturalen Formen. Eine Symbiose dieser beiden Kulturen und ihrer individuellen Designsprache war das erklärte Ziel des Hoteliers Adrian Zecha. Umgesetzt hat er es in Mailand, der Hauptstadt italienischen Designs.

In den öffentlichen Räumen und den 250 Zimmern trifft der Gast auf eine gelungene Kombination aus verführerischer orientalischer Ausstattung mit neoklassischen Elementen. Hier findet sich balinesische Kunst an hell getünchten Wänden, diskret in Szene gesetzt mit indirekter, sanfter Beleuchtung. Prächtige Materialien wie Bronze und Naturstein sowie Mosaike und Keramiken zeigen die asiatischen Einflüsse. Die herbstliche Farbpalette beinhaltet Erdtöne wie Beige, Braun, Ocker und Orange. Im Gegensatz zu den opulent gestalteten öffentlichen Räumlichkeiten, wie der Lobby, dem Restaurant oder dem Spa-Bereich, sind die Zimmer minimalistisch und reduziert gehalten.

IN DESIGNER CIRCLES, Indonesia is famous for its sensual buildings and its striking textiles. Italy, on the other hand, is better known for its revolutionary industrial design and its emphatically sculptural lines. The declared goal of the hotelier, Adrian Zecha, was to achieve a symbiosis of these two cultures and their individual design languages and he has done so in Milan, the capital of Italian design.

In the public spaces and the 250 rooms, the guest finds a successful combination of seductive, oriental furnishing with neoclassical elements. One sees Balinese art on whitewashed walls, discreetly accentuated with indirect, soft lighting, while sumptuous materials such as bronze, natural stone, mosaics and ceramics reveal Asian influences. The autumnal colour scheme contains earthy shades such as beige, brown, ochre and orange. Unlike the opulently furnished spaces such as the lobby, the restaurant or the spa, the rooms are minimalist and restrained.

Address
The Chedi Milan
Via Villapizzone 24
Milan, Italy

Website
www.thechedimilan.com

»at The Chedi« – auch hier im Restaurant verbinden sich Ost und West. Dem Gast werden exklusive italienische Küche und asiatische Kreationen geboten. Hinzu kommt ein umfassendes Weinangebot. // At the restaurant »at The Chedi« too, east and west merge. The guest is served exclusive Italian cuisine and Asian creations, together with a wide-ranging selection of wines.

Im gesamten Hotel setzen verschiedene Lichtarten aparte Akzente. So werden die Tresen der Lobby und der Bar dezent durch Lichtbänder in Szene gesetzt und stimmungsvoller Kerzenschein schmeichelt den Gästen im Restaurant. // Throughout the entire hotel, various types of light create unusual effects. The counters in the lobby and the bar are discreetly accentuated with bands of light, while atmospheric candlelight flatters the diners in the restaurant.

DEUTSCH

ENGLISH

COCO PALM BODU HITHI

Bodu Hithi, Maldives

»EIN PARADIES AUF ERDEN«, so beschreiben Urlauber ihren Aufenthalt im Coco Palm Resort auf der maledivischen Privatinsel Bodu Hithi. Kein Wunder: Die Natur ist atemberaubend schön und die privaten Pavillons laden ein zum Faulenzen, Erholen und Genießen. Es gibt vier verschiedene Villentypen, zwischen 109 und 188 Quadratmeter groß. Die großzügigen Räumlichkeiten sind mit modernen Designermöbeln in hellen, warmen Farben ausgestattet und bieten jeden erdenklichen Luxus. Abgeschirmte, intime Sonnendecks, die zum Teil über einen direkten Zugang zur Lagune verfügen, können zum Relaxen und Sonnen oder auch für ein romantisches Abendessen in einzigartiger Atmosphäre genutzt werden. In den »Island Villas« hat der Gast die Möglichkeit, aus der zentral platzierten Badewanne den direkten Blick auf das türkisblaue Meer zu genießen.

HOLIDAYMAKERS have described their stay at the Coco Palm Resort on the Maldivian private island of Bodu Hithi as »a paradise on earth«. No wonder, given that the surrounding natural world is breathtakingly beautiful and the private pavilions are a standing invitation to laze, rest and enjoy. There are four different types of villa, ranging in size from 1,174 to just over 2,000 square feet. This spacious accommodation is fitted with modern designer furniture in light, warm colours and offers every conceivable luxury. Screened, intimate sun decks, some of which offer direct access to the lagoon, are perfect for relaxing and sunbathing, or also for romantic dining in a unique atmosphere. At the Island Villas, the guest can enjoy the view of the turquoise sea from the centrally placed bathtub.

Address
Coco Palm Bodu Hithi,
North Male Atoll,
Maldives

Website
www.cocopalm.com

Die Fünf-Sterne-Anlage bietet zusätzlich alle Annehmlichkeiten für einen erholsamen Luxus-Urlaub. Dazu gehören exklusive Restaurants und Bars, ein Spa-Bereich sowie ein vielfältiges Yoga- und Wassersportangebot. // This five star resort also offers all amenities for a restful luxury holiday, including exclusive restaurants and bars, a spa and a varied selection of yoga and water sport options.

DEUTSCH

ENGLISH

CHISWICK MORAN HOTEL

London, United Kingdom

AN EINEM BEGRÜNTEN UFER der Themse in West London steht dieses einzigartige Hotel. Der Retro-Chic wird hier liebevoll bis ins Detail zelebriert. Schon in der Lobby wird der Gast darauf eingestimmt. Dunkle Holzvertäfelungen an den Wänden und der grau-weiße Marmorboden bilden die Basis. Teppiche mit grafischen Mustern und Designklassiker lassen die Fünfzigerjahre wiederaufleben. Die Farben sind gedeckt: beige, grau und braun. Ausgewählte Akzente wie ockerfarbene Kissen oder violette Blumenarrangements sind perfekt auf das Ambiente abgestimmt. Auch in den hellen, von Licht durchfluteten Zimmern zeigt sich das Designkonzept: Vorhänge und Stoffe in typischen Mustern und Farben werden geschickt mit modernen Möbeln und Leuchten kombiniert. Das Viersternehotel bietet seinen Gästen zudem einen außergewöhnlichen Komfort: Frühstück, Brunch, Mittagessen, Nachmittagstee, Abendessen oder Snacks – rund um die Uhr kann der Gast bewirtet werden.

THIS UNIQUE HOTEL is situated on the green banks of the Thames in West London, and retro chic is lovingly celebrated here in every detail. This makes itself felt as soon as the guest enters the lobby. Dark wood panelling on the walls and the grey and white marble floor are the starting point. Carpets with graphic patterns and design classics bring the 1950s back to life. The colour scheme is in muted beige, grey and brown. Selected highlights such as ochre-coloured cushions or purple flower arrangements are perfectly in harmony with the ambience. The design concept is also revealed in the bright, sunlit rooms: curtains and textiles with typical patterns and colours are cleverly combined with modern furniture and lighting. This four star hotel also offers its guests an unusual degree of comfort: breakfast, brunch, lunch, afternoon tea, dinner or snacks – the guest is catered to at every hour of the day.

Address
Chiswick Moran Hotel
626 Chiswick High Road
London, UK

Website
www.chiswickhotellondon.co.uk

Das Hotelrestaurant ist einmal mehr ein Kleinod für Retro-Fans: Dunkle Holzmöbel mit hellen grünen Polstern laden zu einem entspannten Essen in einzigartiger Atmosphäre ein. // The hotel restaurant is another little gem for retro fans: with its dark wood furniture upholstered in light green, its unique atmosphere is the ideal place for a relaxed meal.

DEUTSCH

ENGLISH

CUBE BIBERWIER-LERMOOS

Biberwier-Lermoos, Österreich

FUNKTIONALES DESIGN und reduzierte Formensprache prägen die Architektur dieses Hotels. Von außen betrachtet ist das CUBE ein kompakter, würfelförmiger Baukörper, umgeben von einer Glashülle. Modern und zeitgemäß zeigt sich das Design des Interieurs, das durch hinterleuchtete Säulen, Glas, Beton und modernste Möblierung besticht.

Der funktionale Ansatz zieht sich konsequent vom Untergeschoss bis in die letzte Etage durch und manifestiert sich ganz besonders im Rampenkonzept. Die Rampen, auch Gateways genannt, verbinden vom Atrium aus die einzelnen Ebenen miteinander. Die Idee dahinter: Jede Art von Sportgerät muss einfach und mühelos in das Hotelzimmer transportiert werden können, denn im CUBE wird die Sportausrüstung in einem dem Zimmer vorgelagerten Raum aufbewahrt. Im Zimmer wird der konzeptuelle Ansatz fortgesetzt: Das Bett ist eine durchdachte Stahlkonstruktion, als Kasten dient ein verschließbarer Rollcontainer, der unter dem Bett verstaut wird.

Die offene Architektur mit zahlreichen Chill Out Areas fördert die Kommunikation unter den Gästen. Ledersofas vor dem offenen Kamin und Sofawürfel im Atrium der Lobby laden zum Verweilen ein.

THIS HOTEL'S ARCHITECTURE is characterised by functional design and minimalist stylistic vocabulary. Seen from outside, CUBE is a compact, cube-shaped construction surrounded by a glass shell. The interior design is modern and contemporary, charming with back-lit pillars, glass, concrete and the most modern furnishings.

This functional approach is consistently applied from the basement to the top floor and is particularly well displayed in the hotel's ramp concept. The ramps – also known as gateways – connect the individual levels from the atrium. The idea behind this is that it should be possible to transport any kind of sports equipment simply and easily to the rooms, because at the CUBE, each room has an anteroom specially designed for storing sports equipment. In the room, the conceptual approach also prevails. The bed is a well-thought-out steel construction. Storage space is provided in the shape of a lockable container which can be rolled under the bed.

The open architecture with its numerous chill out areas promotes communication amongst the guests. Leather couches in front of the open fireplace and sofa cubes in the lobby's atrium invite the guest to sit for a while.

Address
CUBE
Biberwier-Lermoos
Fernpass-Strasse 71-72
Biberwier-Lermoos,
Austria

Website
www.cube-biberwier.at

Die Glaselemente der Fassade brechen das Licht und spiegeln die spektakuläre Berglandschaft der Alpen. // The façade's glass elements break the light and reflect the spectacular mountain landscape of the Alps.

Kräftige Farben und strenge geometrische Formen bestimmen das Interieur des CUBE. // The interior of the CUBE Hotel is defined by strong colours and austere geometrical shapes.

DEUTSCH

ENGLISH

THE ETON HOTEL

Shanghai, China

STRATEGISCH GÜNSTIG im Herzen des Lujiazui-Finanzdistrikts in Pudong gelegen, erhebt sich das Eton Hotel in den Himmel Shanghais. 460 luxuriöse Zimmer sowie sechs verschiedene Restaurants und Bars beherbergt das imposante Gebäude. Beim Eintritt in das Hotel überkommt den Gast das Gefühl, eine Schatztruhe zu betreten. Dunkles Holz, glänzende Oberflächen und goldene Highlights lassen die Lobby erstrahlen. Alle Zimmer verfügen über einen spektakulären Blick über die Stadt. Die Einrichtung ist klassisch modern; helle zurückhaltende Farben harmonieren mit Akzenten in warmen Braun-, Rot- und Goldtönen. Immer wieder finden sich traditionelle asiatische Muster, Farben und Formen auf Bildern, Wandpaneelen oder als dekorative Elemente. Besonderes Highlight in den Zimmern und Suiten ist das Bad: Badewannen, nur durch eine Glasscheibe vom Zimmer getrennt, und separate Regenduschen vervollständigen das Luxus-Gefühl.

STRATEGICALLY LOCATED in the heart of the Lujiazui financial district in Pudong, the Eton Hotel reaches high into the Shanghai sky. The impressive building houses 460 luxurious rooms as well as six different restaurants and bars. On entering the hotel, the guest is overwhelmed by the feeling of having entered a treasure chest. Dark wood, polished surfaces and golden highlights make the lobby gleam. All of the rooms have a spectacular view of the city. The furnishings are classic modern: light, muted colours harmonise with warm brown, red and gold highlights. One repeatedly encounters traditional Asian patterns, colours and shapes in pictures, wall panels or as decorative elements. The bathrooms are a particular highlight of the rooms and suites: bathtubs, separated from the rooms only by a sheet of glass, and separate rain showers complete the feeling of luxury.

Address
The Eton Hotel
535 Pudong Avenue
Shanghai, China

Website
www.theetonhotel.com

香皂 SOAP
FOAM BATH

Ein Indoor-Pool und ein Garten, der asiatische Elemente mit moderner Landschaftsarchitektur verbindet, runden das Angebot des Business Hotels ab. // This business hotel's amenities are rounded out by an indoor pool and a garden which combines Asian elements with modern landscape architecture.

DEUTSCH

ENGLISH

EVASON ANA MANDARA VILLAS & SIX SENSES SPA

Dalat, Vietnam

IN DEN BERGEN VON DALAT in Vietnam findet sich ein ganz besonderes architektonisches Kleinod: Siebzehn französische Kolonialvillen der Zwanziger- und Dreißigerjahre wurden liebevoll restauriert und bilden jetzt ein außergewöhnliches Resort. Zwei der Villen beherbergen das Restaurant und den großzügigen Spa-Bereich, die übrigen fünfzehn wurden zu Gästehäusern umgestaltet. Entstanden sind 57 Zimmer, alle originalgetreu restauriert und durchströmt vom Charme vergangener Zeiten. Jede Villa verfügt über drei bis fünf Gästezimmer sowie über gemeinschaftlich nutzbare Bereiche, wie einer Lounge mit offenem Kamin, einem Speisezimmer und einer großzügigen Terrasse.

Besondere Highlights sind die Bellevue Suite mit ihrem großzügigen Balkon, der einen 270-Grad-Blick über die spektakuläre Landschaft erlaubt, und die Spa Villa, die in einem kleinen »Chateau« untergebracht ist und über einen eigenen Spa-Bereich und Butlerservice verfügt.

A VERY SPECIAL architectural jewel lies hidden in the Dalat Mountains in Vietnam: seventeen French colonial villas built in the 1920s and 1930s have been lovingly restored and now form a most distinctive resort. Two of the villas house the restaurant and the spacious spa, while the other fifteen have been converted into guest accommodation. A total of 57 rooms have been created, all faithfully restored and exuding the charm of past times. Each villa has three to five guest rooms as well as common areas such as a lounge with open fireplace, dining room and a large terrace.

Particular highlights include the Bellevue Suite with its spacious balcony, offering a 270° view of the spectacular landscape and the Spa Villa, housed in a small »chateau« with its own spa and butler service.

Address
Evason Ana Mandara Villas & Six Senses Spa
Le Lai Street, Ward 5
Dalat, Vietnam

Website
www.sixsenses.com

Ess- und Aufenthaltsräume zeigen sich in apartem Kolonialstil. Dunkles Holz, warme Rottöne und asiatisch anmutende Leuchten prägen die gemeinschaftlichen Bereiche. // Dining and recreation rooms are furnished in striking colonial style. Dark wood, warm red tones and lighting with an Asian touch define the appearance of the common areas.

Bei der Möblierung der Zimmer wurde großer Wert auf originalgetreues Design und Dekor sowie auf zurückhaltende Eleganz gelegt. // With regard to the furnishing of the rooms, great store was placed on faithful design and decor as well as on restrained elegance.

DEUTSCH

ENGLISH

EYNSHAM HALL

Oxfordshire, United Kingdom

DAS UNTER DENKMALSCHUTZ stehende Herrenhaus ist eingebettet in eine wunderschöne Garten- und Parkanlage von über zwölf Hektar. Anfang des 18. Jahrhunderts erbaut, blickt das Gebäude auf eine bewegte Geschichte zurück und hat eine Vielzahl an unterschiedlichsten Bewohnern und Institutionen beherbergt, darunter eine Polizeischule.

Heute ist das Anwesen renoviert und bietet einen luxuriösen Aufenthalt in historischen Gemäuern. Die Einrichtung ist elegant und modern, lässt aber noch hinreichend Raum für den Charme eines ehrwürdigen Landsitzes. Verantwortlich dafür ist die gelungene Mischung aus traditionellen dunklen Holzvertäfelungen, Antiquitäten und modernen Möbeln in hellen Farben und extravaganten Stoffen.

THIS LISTED MANOR HOUSE nestles in over 30 acres of beautiful gardens and parkland. Built at the beginning of the 18th century, the building has a turbulent history and has housed a wide range of inhabitants, including a police training school.

Today the estate has been renovated and offers guests a luxurious stay within historic walls. The furnishings are elegant and modern but leave enough space for the charm of a venerable country manor house to shine through. This has been made possible by the successful mixture of traditional dark wood panelling, antiques and modern furniture in light colours and extravagant materials.

Address
Eynsham Hall
North Leigh, Witney
Oxfordshire, UK

Website
www.eynshamhall.com

Die Gun Room Bar im ehemaligen Waffenzimmer hat für ihr außergewöhnliches Design bereits eine Auszeichnung erhalten: den European Hotel Design Award in der Kategorie »Best Interior Design«. // The Gun Room Bar has already received a European Hotel Design Award in the category »Best Interior Design«.

In den 144 Zimmern herrscht zurückhaltende, kühle Eleganz. Die dunklen Wände stellen einen gelungenen Kontrast zu den Marmorkaminen und der modernen Einrichtung dar. // Restrained, cool elegance dominates in the 144 rooms. The dark walls provide an effective contrast to the marble fireplaces and the modern furnishings.

DEUTSCH

ENGLISH

FÄHRHAUS HOTEL

Sylt, Germany

BEREITS VOR ÜBER 135 JAHREN wurde das Fährhaus Munkmarsch errichtet. Damals war es wohl eine einfache Hafengaststätte für Einheimische und Fischer. Heute gehört das gleichnamige Hotel zu den schönsten auf Sylt und hat mit dem rauen friesischen Charme jener Zeit wenig gemein.

Die Zimmer und Suiten des Gasthauses bieten den Gästen ein einzigartiges Ambiente auf hohem Niveau. Ausgestattet sind die hellen, lichtdurchfluteten Zimmer und Suiten mit einer Mischung aus inseltypischen und modernen Möbelstücken. Sattes, dunkles Holz wird mit zarten Pastelltönen zu einem eleganten Gesamtkonzept kombiniert. Zu dem traditionsreichen Haus gehören auch eine Bibliothek, in der der Gast Bücher und Zeitschriften findet, ein Gourmet-Restaurant sowie ein Spa-Bereich, der keine Wünsche offen lässt.

THE MUNKMARSCH FERRY HOUSE was built over 135 years ago. At the time, it was a simple harbour inn for locals and fishermen. Today the hotel of the same name is one of the most beautiful on the island of Sylt and now has little in common with the rough Freesian charm of those times.

The rooms and suites offer the guests a unique and exclusive ambience. The bright, sunlit rooms and suites are furnished with a mixture of island-typical and modern furniture. Opulent, dark wood is combined with delicate pastel shades to achieve an elegant whole. This longstanding hotel also has a library, stocked with books and magazines, a gourmet restaurant and a spa where the guest's every wish is fulfilled.

Address
Fährhaus Hotel
Heefwai 1
Sylt-Ost/Munkmarsch,
Germany

Website
www.faehrhaus-sylt.de

In der Gaststube finden sich noch die traditionellen blau-weißen Kacheln, die den besonderen Charme des Hotels ausmachen. // The bar is still decorated with traditional blue and white tiles which add to the hotel's special charm.

Vor dem historischen Gebäude kann der Gast bei einer Tasse Kaffee oder einem feinen Essen den Blick auf die herrliche Dünenlandschaft und das Meer genießen. // In front of this historic building, the guest can take a coffee or a fine meal while enjoying the view across the beautiful dune landscape and the sea.

DEUTSCH

ENGLISH

FALCONARA CHARMING HOUSE & RESORT

Falconara, Italy

AN DER SIZILIANISCHEN KÜSTE mit Blick auf das Mittelmeer befindet sich das Falconara Charming House & Resort. Der Komplex in direkter Nachbarschaft zu einer normannischen Festung besteht aus zwei Gebäuden: dem Club House und der Fattoria. Ersteres ist ein neues, modernes Haus; die Fattoria aber ist die einstige Außenstelle der Burg, direkt am Meeresufer gelegen. Raue Natursteinwände, die natürlichen Farbpaletten von Terrakotta und Sandstein sowie die einfachen geometrischen Formen zeugen vom historischen Erbe der Gemäuer. Im Inneren dominieren Stein und Holz. Die schlicht eingerichteten 64 Zimmer und Suiten sind auf beide Gebäude verteilt, die meisten besitzen einen umwerfenden Blick auf das Meer.

Im Club House befindet sich zudem ein luxuriös ausgestatteter Spa-Bereich mit Massageräumen, einem Türkischen Bad und Fitnessgeräten.

THE FALCONARA CHARMING HOUSE & RESORT is situated on the Sicilian coast with a view of the Mediterranean. The complex is immediately adjacent to a Norman fortress comprising two buildings – the Club House and the Fattoria. The first is a new and modern building, while the Fattoria is the former outer structure of the fortress, directly on the seashore. Rough natural stone walls, the earthy colours of terracotta and sandstone and the simple geometrical shapes bear witness to the building's cultural heritage. Inside, stone and wood dominate. The simply furnished 64 rooms and suites are divided over both buildings and most have a stunning view of the sea.

The Club House contains a luxuriously appointed spa with massage rooms, Turkish Bath and fitness equipment.

Address
Falconara Charming House & Resort
Località Falconara
Butera, Sicily, Italy

Website
www.designhotels.com

Nicht nur von außen zeigt sich das Hotel als historisches Gebäude: Auch im Inneren nehmen Details, wie etwa die langen Korridore und die Wände aus Sandstein, auf die historische Kulisse Bezug. // It is not only from outside that one sees the hotel's historic side: the interior too contains details, such as the long corridors and the sandstone walls which make reference to the building's historic past.

DEUTSCH

ENGLISH

THE FORTRESS

Galle, Sri Lanka

WIE EINE GEWALTIGE FESTUNG wirkt das gleichnamige Resort an der Südküste Sri Lankas. Die Architektur ist dem berühmten Fort in Galle nachempfunden. Historische niederländische und portugiesische Stile verbinden sich mit landestypischen Motiven und Designklassikern zu einem innovativen und modernen Ambiente. Direkt an der Küste gelegen, umgeben die Mauern herrliche grüne Gärten, schaukelnde Hängematten, Tagesbetten und atemberaubende Wasserspiele. Auch die 49 luxuriösen und lichtdurchfluteten Zimmer sind von der historischen Kulisse inspiriert. In fünf charakteristische Kategorien unterteilt, kreiert jedes einen sinnlichen Ort mit natürlich-modernen Akzenten. Große Betten, offene Badezimmer und eine technische Ausstattung, die auf dem neuesten Stand ist, gehören zu den Annehmlichkeiten, die den Gast erwarten. Alle Gästezimmer, Lofts und Residenzen sind mit einem privaten Innenhof oder Balkon ausgestattet. Sie bieten fabelhafte Ausblicke auf den prächtigen Garten oder auf den golden schimmernden Strand direkt am Indischen Ozean.

THIS RESORT on Sri Lanka's south coast truly lives up to its name. The architecture is fashioned in the style of the famous Galle Fort. Historic Dutch and Portuguese styles are combined with local motifs and design classics to create an innovative and modern ambience. Directly on the coast, the walls enclose a wonderfully green garden, swinging hammocks, daybeds and breathtaking fountains. The 49 luxurious and light-flooded rooms are also informed by the historical backdrop. They are divided into five characteristic categories, each creating a sensual space with natural, modern accents. Large beds, open bathrooms and the latest technical fittings are amongst the amenities awaiting the guest. All of the rooms, lofts and residences have a private inner courtyard or balcony, offering fantastic views of the spectacular garden or of golden sandbanks right at the edge of the Indian Ocean.

Address
The Fortress
Koggala Beach
Galle, Sri Lanka

Website
www.thefortress.lk

Die Seele baumeln lassen: Die Liegestühle am Meeresufer zwischen meterhohen Palmen sind der perfekte Ort zum Entspannen. // Give your spirit a rest: the loungers at the edge of the sea, between sky-high palms, are the perfect place to relax.

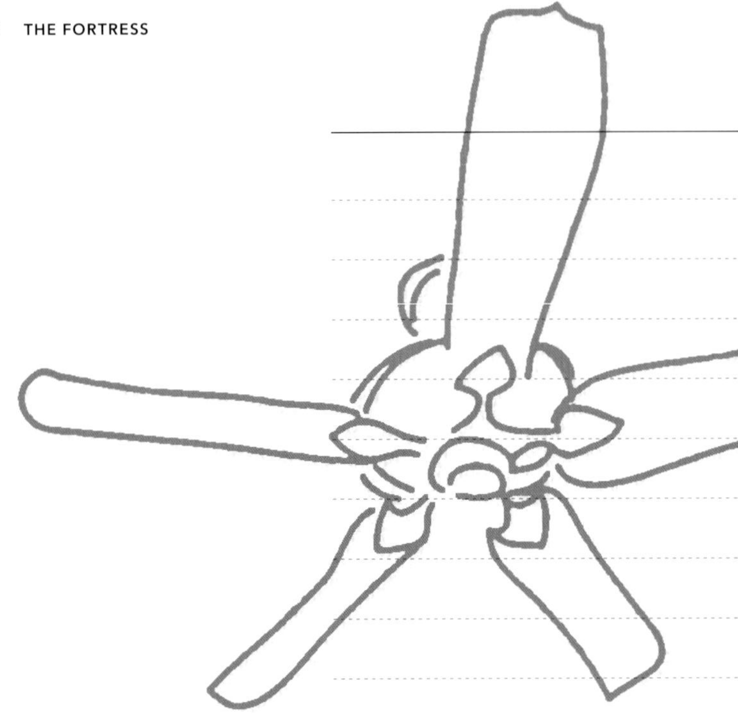

Verschiedene Restaurants und Bars servieren einheimische Küche, internationale Speisen und eine Vielzahl exotischer Cocktails. // Various restaurants and bars serve local cuisine, international dishes and a wide range of exotic cocktails.

In einigen Zimmern gehören private Pools zur Ausstattung. Sie bieten dem verwöhnten Gast einen ganz besonderen Luxus. // Some of the rooms have their own private pool, offering the pampered guest that little extra luxury.

Die Sea Lounge ist der perfekte Ort, um unter funkelndem Sternenhimmel einen mit landestypischem Tee zubereiteten Cocktail zu genießen. // The Sea Lounge is the perfect spot to enjoy a local tea cocktail under a twinkling, starry sky.

In der Nacht wird das herrschaftliche Gebäude durch perfekt inszenierte Beleuchtung in Szene gesetzt. Die großen Fenster lassen den Blick in die prächtige Lobby und die Treppenaufgänge frei. // At night, this imposing building stands centre stage with perfectly placed lighting. The large windows give a free view of the sumptuous lobby and staircases.

DEUTSCH

ENGLISH

FARNHAM ESTATE HOTEL

Farnham, Ireland

MONDÄN, LUXURIÖS UND STYLISCH – so präsentiert sich das Farnham Estate Hotel. Das Haus im georgianischen Stil, dessen Grundmauern aus dem 16. Jahrhundert stammen, befindet sich auf einem über 500 Hektar großen Landsitz und gilt als eines der schönsten Resorts Irlands. Sein Interieur ist eine gelungene Mischung aus historisch anmutenden Möbeln und zeitgemäßem Design. Die Sofas und Sessel scheinen einer anderen Zeit zu entstammen: klassisch elegante Formen, gedeckte Farben. Doch in den Details wird das Gestaltungskonzept sichtbar: Tapeten- oder Stoffmuster mit floralen Motiven sind modern interpretiert, Sessel wurden mit goldenem Leder überzogen und klare geometrische Formen bestimmen die Architektur.

Die 146 Zimmer und vier der insgesamt zwölf Suiten des Hotels sind im modernen Flügel untergebracht. Hier besticht die luxuriöse Ausstattung durch raffinierte Farbkompositionen, die die Farben des Gartens und der umgebenden Landschaft widerspiegeln. Weitere acht Suiten befinden sich im historischen Landhaus. Sie alle wurden aufwendig restauriert und lassen den Charme irischer Adelssitze wieder spürbar werden.

THE FARNHAM ESTATE HOTEL presents itself as sophisticated, luxurious and stylish. This Georgian house, whose original structure dates back to the 16th century, is on an estate of over 1,300 acres and is considered to be one of Ireland's most beautiful resorts. The interior is a successful mix of antique style furniture and contemporary design. The sofas and armchairs seem to come from another era in classic, elegant shapes and muted colours. But the design concept becomes apparent in the details: wallcoverings or textiles with floral patterns have been given a modern twist; armchairs are upholstered in gold leather and clean geometrical shapes define the architecture.

The 146 rooms and four of the twelve suites are housed in a modern wing. Here the luxurious furnishings captivate through their clever use of colour, which reflects the colours of the garden and the surrounding landscape. A further eight suites are located in the historic manor house. They have all been fully restored and embody the charm of the Irish gentry house.

Address
Farnham Estate Hotel
Farnham Estate
Cavan, Irland

Website
www.farnhamestate.ie

Feine Baumstämme und Äste zieren die extravagante Tapete des Kaminzimmers. // The extravagant wallcoverings in the fireplace room are ornamented with fine tree trunks and branches.

DEUTSCH

ENGLISH

FIRST HOTEL GRIMS GRENKA

Oslo, Norway

DAS FÜNFSTERNEHOTEL GRIMS GRENKA, mitten in Oslos City, ist ein Lifestyle-Experiment: Hier wird modernistisches Design mit einem innovativen Nachtclub, internationaler Fusion-Küche und einer Rooftop Lounge geschickt gemixt. Die 42 Zimmer und 24 Suiten des Hotels bestechen durch ihr klares Design. Dunkles Holz, hochflorige Teppiche und anthrazitgraue Backsteinwände werden in den Zimmern von verschiedenen farblichen Akzenten begleitet. Warmes Rot, sommerliches Grün, winterliches Blau und Weiß oder dekadente Highlights in Gold setzen die Räumlichkeiten gekonnt in Szene. Gezielt platzierte, indirekte Leuchten hüllen die langen Räume in sanftes, beruhigendes Licht. Abgerundet wird die Innenraumgestaltung durch den opulenten Einsatz von Holz und anderen Naturmaterialien in den großzügigen Badezimmern.

THE FIVE STAR GRIMS GRENKA, in the middle of Oslo, is a lifestyle experiment. Modernist design is cleverly mixed with an innovative nightclub, international fusion cuisine and a rooftop lounge. The clean design of the hotel's 42 rooms and 24 suites is enchanting. Dark wood, deep pile carpets and anthracite grey brick walls are accompanied in the rooms by various colour accents: warm red, summery green, wintery blue and white or decadent gold highlights effectively complement the rooms. Carefully placed indirect illumination bathes the long rooms in a soft, calming light. The room design is rounded out with the opulent use of wood and other natural materials in the spacious bathrooms.

Address
First Hotel Grims Grenka
Kongens gate 5
Oslo, Norway

Website
www.firsthotels.com
www.grimsgrenka.no

Ein Fadenvorhang trennt Bereiche in den Zimmern ab und schafft eine intime Atmosphäre mit Blick auf die Altstadt Oslos. //
A thread curtain separates different areas of the room and creates an intimate atmosphere with a view across Oslo's old town.

Frei stehende Betten oder Badewannen verstärken das Gefühl von Weite und Raum. // Freestanding beds and bathtubs further enhance the sense of breadth and space.

DEUTSCH

ENGLISH

GERBERMÜHLE

Frankfurt am Main, Germany

DIE FRANKFURTER GERBERMÜHLE ist ein traditionsreiches Gebäude und wurde nun nach ausgiebigen Renovierungsarbeiten zu einem kleinen, besonderen Hotel umgebaut. Entstanden ist ein stilecht und geschmackvoll miteinander verbundener Komplex, der Tradition und Innovation zu einer Einheit verschmelzen lässt: alte Werte in Kombination mit zeitgemäßem Design. Und das alles direkt am Ufer des Mains, umgeben von einer malerischen Landschaft und direkt vor der imposanten Skyline Frankfurts.

Bereits im 14. Jahrhundert stand an der Stelle des heutigen Gebäudes ein Lehngut. Im 16. Jahrhundert wurde die Getreidemühle errichtet, und knapp einhundert Jahre später wurde dieser Ort als Gerberei genutzt. Der Name ist bis heute erhalten geblieben und steht nun für Individualität und persönlichen Service im historischen Ambiente.

FRANKFURT'S GERBERMÜHLE is a venerable building and, following painstaking renovation, has now been converted into a small and special hotel. What has been created is a tastefully linked complex with authentic style, in which tradition and innovation are completely merged – old values combined with contemporary design. And all of this directly on the banks of the River Main, surrounded by a picturesque landscape and immediately adjacent to Frankfurt's imposing skyline.

A fief already existed on the site of the present building in the 14th century. In the 16th century a grain mill was erected and almost one hundred years later, the site became a tannery. This latter activity is recalled in the building's name, which it still bears today. Today the new Gerbermühle represents personal service in a historic atmosphere.

Address
Gerbermühle
Gerbermühlstrasse 105
Frankfurt am Main,
Germany

Website
www.gerbermuehle.de

Elegante, exklusive Möbel und sanfte Farbspiele runden das luxuriöse Gesamtbild der Hotelzimmer ab. // Elegant, exclusive furniture and the gentle play of colour round out the luxurious overall picture of the rooms.

Die Zimmer verfügen über alle Annehmlichkeiten, die anspruchsvolle Gäste von einem modernen Hotel erwarten dürfen. Die fünf Suiten sind allesamt Unikate mit dezenten Hinweisen auf die architektonische Nachbarschaft zu den erhaltenen historischen Elementen. // All rooms are equipped with every conceivable amenity which the discriminating guest expects from a modern hotel. The five suites are all different, discreetly indicating their architectural proximity to the preserved historic elements.

GOETHE

A
IN DER GEBORGENHEIT, IM GEFÄNGNIS EINES
GESCHICHTE SIND SIE ANEINANDER MIT ANDEREN GEKETTET.
SCHÖN UND GRAUSAM ZUGLEICH. DIE NÄHE DES ANDEREN
FLUCHT. LEISES WEGSCHLEICHEN. NICHT ERSCHEINEN.
HEBENDE UND SINKENDE FEDERDECKEN LASSEN DIE PAARUNG
EROTISCH ERSCHEINEN. JA, SIE HABEN SICH WEG
VIELLEICHT WAREN SIE ABER GAR NOCH NICHT IM
A SCHEINT ZU SCHNELL. TREIBT SEIN LINKER BALKEN SICH
WEISS B EIGENTLICH WAS ES DA EMPFÄNGT?
ERSCHEINEN KÖNNEN? ALS KLEINES A VIELLEICHT, RUND UND
SEINE KANTEN IM KISSEN. DAS WILLENLOS

DEUTSCH

ENGLISH

N TEXTES, EINES ROMANS, EINER
ILE ZU ZEILE WÄCHST DAS BEGEHREN.
HLEN FAST SCHMECKEN ZU KÖNNEN.
E SÜSSE DUNKELHEIT.
BUCHSTABEN DANN EHER KOMISCH ALS
HEN. AUS DEN WÖRTERN.
AHER DIE UNBEHOLFENHEIT.
WIE EIN KEIL IN DIE HÜFTE VON B?
A NICHT EIN WENIG ANDERS
DIG? B INDES VERSTECKT
E?

GOLDMAN 25HOURS

Frankfurt am Main, Germany

ZEITGEMÄSSES DESIGN, ein individueller Stil und guter Service zu moderaten Übernachtungspreisen: Dieses Konzept findet sich beim 25hours überall wieder. Die 95 Zimmer und sieben Suiten, davon zwei in XL, sind außergewöhnlich und mit viel Liebe zum Detail gestaltet. Möbel junger Designer werden mit Klassikern zu einem harmonischen Ensemble kombiniert. Großflächige Grafiken, ungewöhnliche Kurztexte oder Retro-Tapeten zieren die Wände der Zimmer und öffentlichen Räumlichkeiten. Die Zimmer und Studios im 25hours bieten Raum und Freiheit, unaufdringlich klaren Stil und ein Maximum an Wandlungsfähigkeit. Der Kamin im so genannten Wohnzimmer lädt den Gast ein, einen Moment zu verweilen.

CONTEMPORARY DESIGN, an individual style and good service at reasonable prices: this concept is repeated throughout 25hours. The 95 rooms and seven suites, two of which are XL, are extraordinary, designed with a great eye for detail. Furniture from young designers is combined with classic pieces to create a harmonious ensemble. Large-scale graphics, unusual pieces of text or retro wallpaper decorate the walls in both the rooms and the public spaces. The rooms and studios at 25hours offer space and freedom, unobtrusive, clear style and maximum transformability. The fireplace in the so-called Living Room is an open invitation for guests to spend some time there.

Address
Goldman 25hours
Hanauer Landstrasse 127
Frankfurt am Main,
Germany

Website
www.25hours-hotels.com

Besonderes Ambiente bietet das stilvolle Restaurant mit kleiner Küche und Bar. Hier werden wechselnde Kreationen aus deutscher und italienischer Küche angeboten. //
This stylish restaurant with its little kitchen and bar has a very special ambience. It offers regularly changing creations based on German and Italian cuisine.

A smile is the prettiest
thing you can wear.
LOUNGE

Einzigartige Designobjekte und Grafiken geben jedem Zimmer seinen besonderen Charme. // Unique designer objects and graphics give each room its particular charm.

Ob ungezwungenes »Get-together« oder große Empfänge, das Wohnzimmer ist immer der passende Ort. Im angrenzenden »Meet & Eat«-Bereich mit langer Bar kann das dazugehörige Catering dekorativ angerichtet werden. // Whether for relaxed get togethers or for big receptions, the Living Room is always the ideal spot. Event catering can be arranged decoratively in the adjacent Meet & Eat area with its long bar.

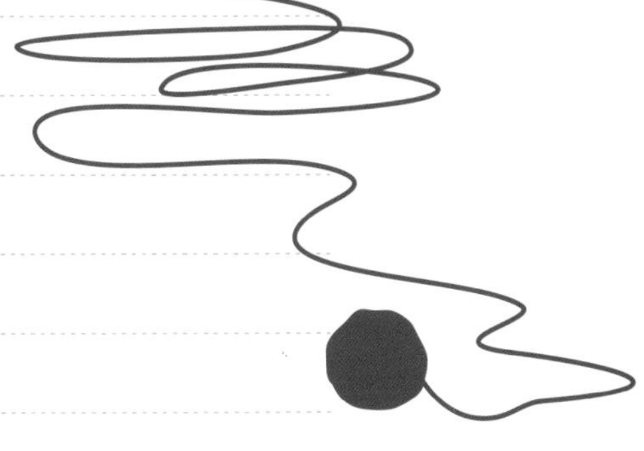

DEUTSCH

ENGLISH

GRAMERCY PARK HOTEL

New York City, USA

DAS GRAMERCY PARK ist bereits seit seiner Eröffnung im Jahr 1925 ein ganz besonderer Ort. Erbaut von Robert T. Lyons, war es immer Anlaufpunkt der High Society und der Boheme und hat bereits viele Berühmtheiten beherbergt. Hier heiratete Humphrey Bogart seine erste Frau Helen Menken, an der Bar tranken schon die Mitglieder der englischen Kultband Babe Ruth oder Joe Strummer von The Clash. Um diesen Glanz, trotz Modernisierung und Umbau, beizubehalten, wurden originale Elemente mit zeitgemäßen Akzenten stilvoll kombiniert.

Schon beim Eintritt in das historische Gebäude beeindruckt die imposante Lobby: Die sechs Meter hohen Decken werden von ebenso großen Säulen aus Douglasie gehalten, die Wände erstrahlen in warmem Grau, schwarz-weiße marokkanische Fliesen schmücken den Boden, schwere Samtvorhänge halten das hektische Treiben draußen und ein prachtvoller venezianischer Leuchter sorgt für das richtige Licht. Besonderes Highlight ist der drei Meter hohe Kamin, der speziell für diesen Raum von Julian Schnabel entworfen wurde.

Und auch in den 185 Zimmern wird Kunst großgeschrieben: Bilder der berühmtesten Fotografen der Agentur Magnum zieren die Wände.

SINCE ITS OPENING IN 1925, the Gramercy Park has been a very special hotel. Built by Robert T. Lyons, it was always a meeting place for high society and bohemians and has seen many prominent guests in its time. This is where Humphrey Bogart married his first wife, Helen Menken. The bar has entertained members of the English cult band, Babe Ruth, and Joe Strummer of The Clash. In order to preserve this glamour, modernisation and conversion notwithstanding, original elements have been combined with contemporary accents.

The visitor is immediately impressed by this historic building's imposing lobby: the almost 20 foot high ceilings are supported by huge pillars of Douglas fir, the walls glow in warm grey, black and white Moroccan tiles decorate the floor, heavy velvet curtains keep out the hectic bustle on the streets and a magnificent Venetian chandelier provides the right lighting. One particular highlight is the ten foot high fireplace which was specially designed for this room by Julian Schnabel.

Each of the 185 rooms in the hotel is unique. Art is also written large here with works by the Magnum agency's most famous photographers decorating the walls.

Address
Gramercy Park Hotel
2 Lexington Avenue
New York City, USA

Website
www.gramercyparkhotel.com

Neben den Werken des für das Gesamtkonzept und die Art Direktion zuständigen Künstlers Julian Schnabel finden sich in diesem einzigartigen Haus Kunstobjekte von Andy Warhol, Cy Twombly, Jean-Michel Basquiat, Damien Hirst und Richard Prince. // Alongside the works of the artist responsible for the overall concept and art direction, Julian Schnabel, this unique hotel also contains works by Andy Warhol, Cy Twombly, Jean-Michel Basquiat, Damien Hirst and Richard Prince.

DEUTSCH

ENGLISH

GRAND HOTEL CENTRAL

Barcelona, Spain

HEKTISCH, LAUT UND OFT SEHR HEISS – so ist es in der spanischen Metropole Barcelona. Es gibt aber auch Oasen der Ruhe. Eine von ihnen ist das Grand Hotel Central. In einem denkmalgeschützten Prachtbau aus dem Jahr 1926 kann sich der Besucher von der flirrenden Stadt zurückziehen und zur Ruhe kommen.

Schon im Eingangsbereich strahlt das Hotel seinen besonderen Charme aus. Der ursprüngliche Steinboden, schmiedeeiserne Treppengeländer sowie Eisenlüster erinnern an vergangene Zeiten. Kombiniert wird die prachtvolle Ausstattung mit farblich abgestimmten, avantgardistischen Möbeln und Stoffen. Korridore und Treppenhäuser wurden bewusst mit dicken Teppichen und dunklen Tapeten ausgestattet.

Auch in den 147 Zimmern und Suiten kann der Gast Stille und Entspannung genießen. Das dezente Farbspiel der Wände, Böden und Möbel in sanften Beige- und Brauntönen mit dem strahlenden Weiß der frisch gestärkten Laken harmoniert hervorragend mit den klaren Formen. Dunkelbraune Stoffrollos halten die grelle Sonne ab und tauchen das Zimmer in warmes Licht.

HECTIC, LOUD AND OFTEN VERY HOT – that's the way it is in the Spanish metropolis of Barcelona. But there are also oases of tranquillity, one of which is the Grand Hotel Central. Located in a magnificent listed building erected in 1926, the visitor can retreat from the frenetic bustle of the city and unwind.

On entering the lobby, one is immediately struck by the hotel's charm. The original stone flooring, cast-iron balustrades and iron chandeliers evoke the spirit of times past. The sumptuous furnishings are combined with colour-coordinated avant garde furniture and textiles. Corridors and stairways have deliberately been fitted with thick carpets and dark wallcoverings.

The guest can also enjoy peace and relaxation in the 147 rooms. The discreet colours of the walls, floors and furniture in gentle beige and brown tones and the gleaming white of the freshly starched bed linen combine perfectly with the clean lines. Dark brown textile blinds keep out the glaring sun and bathe the room in a warm light.

Address
Grand Hotel Central
Via Layetana, 30
Barcelona, Spain

Website
www.grandhotelcentral.com

Frühstück, Mittagessen, Abendessen oder nur ein paar Tapas zwischendurch: Das Restaurant Actual bietet einfallsreiche, frische und mediterrane Küche von Starkoch Ramón Freixa. // Breakfast, lunch, dinner or just a few tapas in between: the Actual Restaurant offers creative, fresh Mediterranean cuisine from the star chef, Ramón Freixa.

Ein besonderes Highlight ist der atemberaubende Pool auf dem Dach, der ausschließlich den Gästen vorbehalten ist. Von hier reicht der Blick über die Dächer der Stadt hin zu den historischen Sehenswürdigkeiten, wie die Kathedrale oder die zwei berühmten Hochhäuser am Jachthafen der Stadt. //
A particular highlight however is the breathtaking pool on the roof, which is exclusively reserved for hotel guests. From here one has a view across the city's roofs, taking in the historic sights such as the Cathedral or the two famous skyscrapers at the yacht harbour.

In der Bibliothek kann der Gast in Stadtführern oder in Kunst-, Design- und Architekturbildbänden blättern oder seinen Tag planen. // In the library, guests can leaf through books on the city, art, design and architecture or make plans for the day.

DEUTSCH

ENGLISH

HOSPES VILLA PAULITA

Puigcerdà, Spain

EHEMALS EINE SOMMERRESIDENZ in Familienbesitz, hat sich die Hospes Villa Paulita in ein Kleinod für Naturliebhaber verwandelt. Sie liegt direkt am See von Puigcerdà am Rande der katalanischen Pyrenäen und bietet sich zu jeder Jahreszeit als ideale Unterkunft an: im Frühjahr, Sommer und Herbst als Basis für Wanderungen oder Kultur-Erkundungen, im Winter als Skihotel. Die aus dem 19. Jahrhundert stammende Villa wurde durch zwei neue Anbauten erweitert.

Die öffentlichen Räume sowie die 34 individuell gestalteten Zimmer und vier Suiten verteilen sich gleichmäßig auf die drei Gebäude. Designerleuchten, moderne Möbel und Stoffe in Creme und Silber fügen sich perfekt in die historische Umgebung ein. Dazu gehören Holzbalkendecken, schmiedeeiserne Geländer, Buntglasfenster und ausgesuchte Antiquitäten.

ONCE A FAMILY-OWNED SUMMER RESIDENCE, the Hospes Villa Paulita has been transformed into a little treasure for nature lovers. It is situated directly on Lake Puigcerdà at the edge of the Catalonian Pyrenees and offers perfect accommodation all year round. In spring, summer and autumn it is ideal as a base for walking or cultural exploration, while in winter it serves as a ski hotel. The villa, built in the 19th century, has been extended with two new annexes.

The public spaces, as well as the 34 individually designed rooms and four suites are evenly distributed over the three buildings. Designer lighting, modern furniture and textiles in cream and silver blend in perfectly with their historic surroundings which include wooden beamed ceilings, cast-iron balustrades, stained glass windows and choice antiques.

Address
Hospes Villa Paulita
Av. Pons i Gasch, 15
Puigcerdà, Spain

Website
www.hospes.es

Der Spa-Bereich im unteren Teil des Resorts ist dank der Glaspyramiden im Innenhof von Tageslicht durchflutet. // Thanks to the glass pyramid in the inner courtyard, the spa area in the lower part of the resort is flooded with daylight.

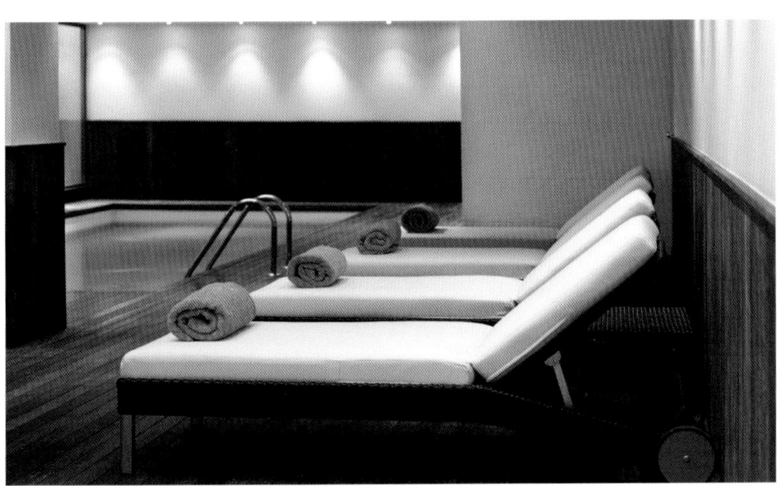

DEUTSCH

ENGLISH

HYATT REGENCY HAKONE RESORT & SPA

Hakone, Japan

IM HYATT REGENCY Hakone Resort & Spa residieren Gäste am Fuße des Fuji-Hakone-Izu-Nationalparks in Gora, einer für ihre natürlichen Thermalquellen bekannten Gegend. Die ruhige Lage mit gepflegter Gartenanlage und Panoramablick heißt den Gast willkommen, sobald er die geräumige Lobby betritt. In allen Räumlichkeiten werden traditionelle japanische Elemente auf moderne, luxuriöse Weise stilvoll in Szene gesetzt. Im »Wohnzimmer« erwartet den Gast eine zentral platzierte offene Feuerstelle, um die sich gepolsterte Sitzgelegenheiten gruppieren. Der außergewöhnlich hohe Raum sorgt mit seinem harmonischen Farbspiel in Braun- und Rottönen für eine behagliche Atmosphäre.

Jedes der 79 Hotelzimmer ist mit weichen Decken und Bezügen, einem Arbeitsbereich mit Highspeed-Internetzugang, einem luxuriösen Badezimmer und einem privaten Balkon beziehungsweise einer privaten Veranda ausgestattet. In einigen Zimmern und Suiten finden sich zudem Bereiche, die mit Tatami-Matten ausgelegt sind und zu einem traditionellen Essen einladen.

AT THE HYATT REGENCY Hakone Resort & Spa, guests reside at the foot of Fuji Hakone Izu National Park in Gora, a region famous for its natural thermal springs. This tranquil dwelling with its carefully tended gardens and panorama view makes the guest welcome as soon as he enters the spacious lobby. All of the rooms are stylishly presented using traditional Japanese elements with a modern, luxurious twist. In the »living room« a centrally placed open fireplace, around which cushioned seating has been grouped, awaits the guest. The exceptionally high room, harmoniously decorated in brown and red tones, has a most comfortable atmosphere.

Each of the 79 hotel rooms is fitted with soft blankets and linen, a working area with high speed internet access, a luxurious bathroom and a private balcony or veranda. Some of the rooms and suites also contain spaces laid out with tatami mats, ideal for enjoying a traditional meal.

Address
Hyatt Regency Hakone Resort & Spa
Gora Hakone-machi, Ashigarashimo-gun
Hakone, Kanagawa Prefecture, Japan

Website
hakone.regency.hyatt.com

Natürliche Materialien, schlichte Formen und dezente Farben sorgen in den Gästezimmern für ein Gefühl der Besinnung und Entspannung im Einklang mit der japanischen Philosophie. // Natural materials, simple lines and muted colours in the guest rooms provide a feeling of contemplation and relaxation in keeping with Japanese philosophy.

Als Refugium bietet sich das Izumi Spa an: Hier finden die Gäste bei ganzheitlichen Behandlungen und in den natürlichen Thermalquellen (Onsen) von Hakone Ruhe, Körperharmonie und inneres Gleichgewicht. // Guests can also retreat to the Izumi Spa, where they can enjoy holistic treatments and achieve peace, physical harmony and inner balance through a dip in the Hakone's Onsen or natural thermal springs.

DEUTSCH

ENGLISH

HOTEL DE ROME

Berlin, Germany

BIS ZUM ENDE DES ZWEITEN WELTKRIEGS war das 1889 von Ludwig Heim entworfene Stadtpalais Sitz einer großen Bank. Heute erstrahlt das historische Gebäude in neuem Glanz und beherbergt ein atemberaubendes Luxushotel. Das prachtvolle Interieur, in dem neoklassische Elemente mit einer zeitgemäßen Einrichtung aus Stahl und Glas verwoben sind, lockt Gäste aus aller Welt an. Zwei knallrot lackierte und extragroße Kopien von Farnese-Vasen aus den Kapitolinischen Museen schmücken den Eingangsbereich.

Das Hotel beherbergt 101 großzügig geschnittene Zimmer und 45 Suiten. Die Präsidentensuite besitzt eine spektakuläre Terrasse, die sich über die gesamte Länge des Baus erstreckt. Alle Zimmer verfügen über hohe Decken und klassische Proportionen. Auch die Einrichtung ist klassisch-elegant gehalten: dezente Farben und reduzierte Formen dominieren. Farbakzente in Rot, extravagante Kunstobjekte und außergewöhnliche Einzelstücke offerieren interessante Ein- und Ausblicke. Die mit Marmor verkleideten Badezimmer bieten mit separaten Duschen und frei stehenden Badewannen ein hohes Maß an Luxus.

UP TO THE END OF THE SECOND WORLD WAR, the city palace built in 1889 by Ludwig Heim was the headquarters of a large bank. Today this historic building has been restored in all its glory and houses an astonishing luxury hotel. The sumptuous interior which combines neoclassical elements with contemporary steel and glass furnishings, draws visitors from all over the world. On entering, the guest is immediately struck by the two bright red lacquered, outsize reproductions of the Farnese Vases in the Capitoline Museums.

The Hotel de Rome has 101 generously sized rooms and 45 suites. The Presidential Suite has a spectacular terrace extending over the full length of the building. All of the rooms have high ceilings and classic proportions. The furnishings too are classic and elegant: subdued colours and clean lines dominate. Interesting insights and glimpses are created with red highlights, extravagant works of art and unusual one-off pieces. The marble-tiled bathrooms are particularly luxurious with separate showers and freestanding bathtubs.

Address
Hotel de Rome
Behrenstrasse 37
Berlin, Germany

Website
www.hotelderome.com

Schon in der Lobby wird der Gast atmosphärisch auf das mondäne Innenleben des Fünfsternehotels eingestimmt. // The atmosphere in the lobby already prepares the guest for the sophisticated inner life of this five star hotel.

DEUTSCH

ENGLISH

HAYMARKET HOTEL

London, United Kingdom

DIESES HOTEL in der englischen Hauptstadt hebt sich auf erfrischende Weise von den üblichen minimalistischen Designhotels ab. Farbenfrohe moderne Möbel, Stoffe und Anstriche werden in ungewöhnlicher Weise in die klassische Kulisse dieses Stadthauses integriert. Die Fassade des nahe dem Trafalgar Square gelegenen Hotels wurde Anfang des 19. Jahrhunderts von dem britischen Architekten John Nash entworfen. Frisch renoviert beherbergt das Gebäude nun 50 exklusive Gästezimmer.

Die Zimmer bestechen durch ihren individuellen Charakter. Es gibt Räume, die dezent in Schwarz und Weiß akzentuiert sind, in anderen sind Polster und Betten mit großflächigen gelben Blumenstoffen bezogen. Allen gemein ist jedoch der humorvolle Umgang mit klassischen Elementen und deren Neuinterpretation durch knallige Farben oder ungewöhnliche Muster. Extravagante Drucke, Bilder und Skulpturen unterstreichen die Einzigartigkeit der Räumlichkeiten.

THIS HOTEL in the English capital is refreshingly different from minimalist design hotels. Colourful modern furniture, textiles and paints are integrated into the classical backdrop of this townhouse in an unusual way. The façade of this hotel, located close to Trafalgar Square, was designed by the British architect, John Nash, at the beginning of the 19th century. Newly renovated, the building now contains 50 exclusive guest rooms.

The individual character of the rooms makes them most attractive. There are rooms discreetly accented with black and white, while in others, large print yellow floral textiles have been used for the upholstery and beds. What all rooms have in common is their humorous treatment of classic elements and their reinterpretation with vibrant colours or unusual patterns. Extravagant prints, pictures and sculptures underline the unique quality of the rooms.

Address
Haymarket Hotel
1 Suffolk Place
London, UK

Website
www.firmdale.com

Poppige Fotos auf großflächig bedruckten Stoffen und Tapeten dominieren das Restaurant BRUMUS. // The BRUMUS restaurant is dominated by lively prints on large-scale printed textiles and wallcoverings.

Die Gäste können den 18 Meter langen Pool mit Bar und einem Soundsystem, das dem eines Nachtclubs ebenbürtig ist, nutzen. // Guests have the use of a 59 feet pool with bar and a sound system which is the equal of any to be found in a nightclub.

Das Design dieses Zimmers interpretiert traditionelle englische Muster und Eigenheiten. Streifen in kräftigem Türkis wirken wie mit Filzstift auf die Wand gemalt. Einzelne Möbel und »tierische« Bilder an den Wänden setzen Akzente in kontrastreichen Pink- und Rottönen. // The design of this room is based on an interpretation of traditional English patterns and idiosyncracies. Stripes in bold turquoise resemble strokes of a felt tip pen on the wall. Individual pieces of furniture and striking pictures on the walls create contrast-rich pink and red highlights.

Schon in der Lobby wird das Innenraumkonzept deutlich: Die Wandgestaltungen und die Möblierung bestechen durch ihr dezentes Farbspiel in Schwarz, Weiß, Grau sowie Akzenten in kräftigem Zitronengelb. Skulpturen und großformatige Kunstwerke ergänzen dieses außergewöhnliche Ambiente. // In the lobby, the interior room concept is already apparent: the wall decorations and furnishings are pleasing with their subdued interplay of black, white and grey, with touches of zingy lemon yellow. This unusual ambience is complemented by sculptures and large-scale works of art.

Kräftige Farben sowie großflächige Muster auf Tapeten und Stoffen kombiniert mit klassischen Möbeln machen jedes Zimmer zu einem Unikat. // Strong colours and large patterns on wallcoverings and textiles, combined with classic furniture, make each room unique.

DEUTSCH

J. K. PLACE

Capri, Italy

IN HEKTISCHEN ZEITEN braucht der Mensch einen Platz, an dem er zur Ruhe kommen kann. Ein solcher Ort ist das J. K. Place auf der Insel Capri. Die Geschichte dieses Hauses geht zurück auf die 1878 erbaute Villa Bovaro, die erstmals 1885 in ein Hotel umgewandelt wurde. Es war in der Hand verschiedener Besitzer und hat eine Vielzahl an berühmten Gästen beherbergt. Direkt an der Mittelmeerküste gelegen, versprüht es auch heute noch seinen mediterranen Charme. In den Räumlichkeiten dominieren die Farben der Insel: Blau und Weiß. Klassische Möbel und typische Dekorationen aus der maritimen Umgebung ergeben ein harmonisches, elegantes Bild. Von fast jedem Zimmer aus ist der Blick auf das strahlend blaue Wasser zu genießen.

Auch das Restaurant mit seiner sich zum Meer hin öffnenden Terrasse hat sich den traditionellen, mediterranen Genüssen verschrieben.

ENGLISH

WHEN IT'S HECTIC, a person needs a place to unwind. One such place is the hotel J. K. Place on Capri. The history of this hotel dates back to the Villa Bovaro, built in 1878, which was first converted into a hotel in 1885. It has had various owners and housed a huge number of famous guests. Located directly on the Mediterranean coast, it still exudes southern charm. The rooms are dominated by the colours of the island – blue and white. Classic furniture and typical decorations inspired by this maritime environment create a harmonious, elegant picture. A view of the sparkling, blue water can be enjoyed from nearly all the rooms.

The restaurant too, with its terrace open to the sea, has also dedicated itself to traditional, Mediterranean pleasures.

Address
J. K. Place
Via Prov. Marina Grande
Capri, Italy

Website
www.jkplace.com

Bis ins kleinste Detail liebevoll dekoriert, vermittelt das J. K. Place das Gefühl, zu Gast bei Freunden zu sein. // Lovingly decorated down to the smallest detail, the J. K. Place gives one the feeling of staying with friends.

THE KENNEDYS
THE HOME MODERNISED

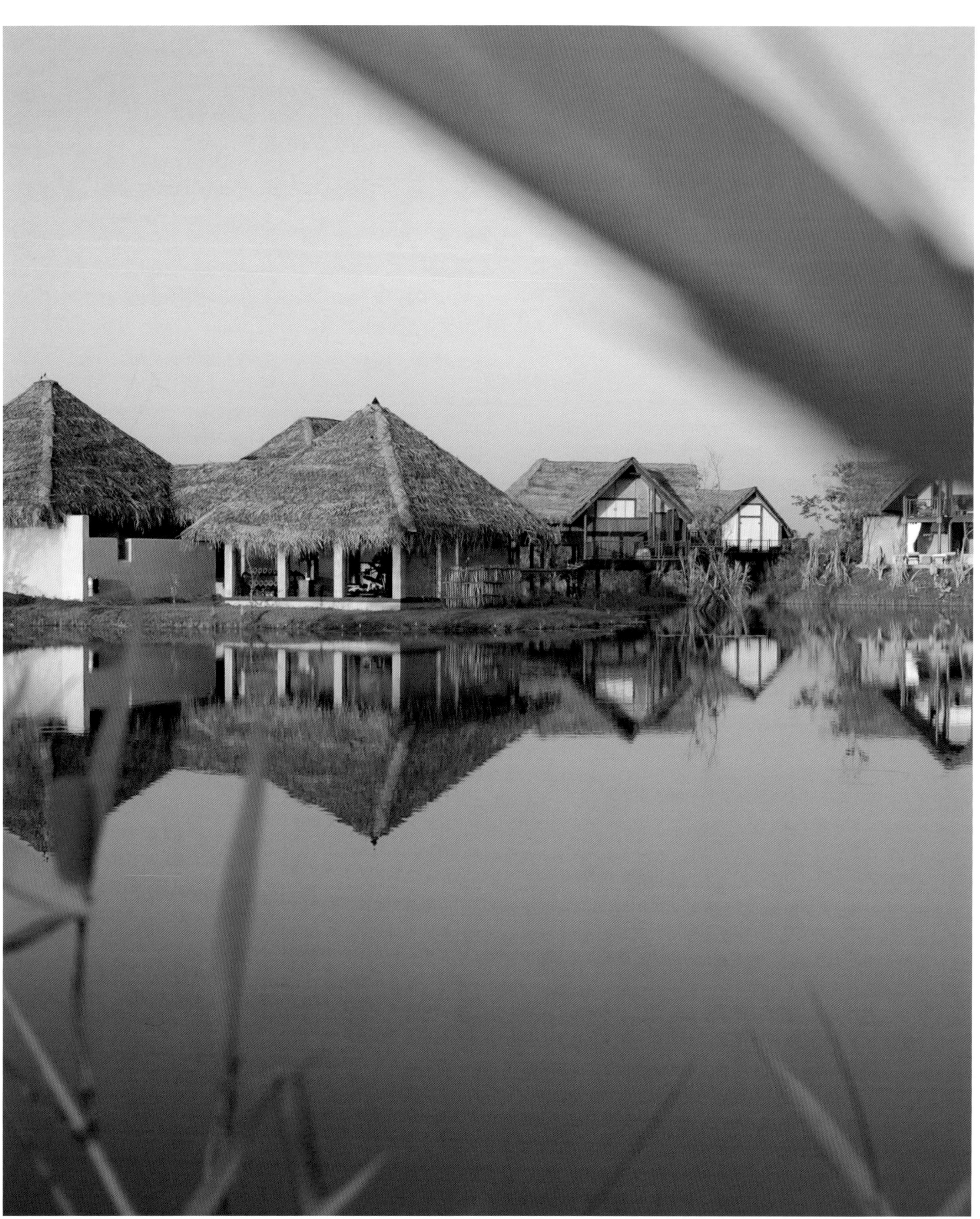

DEUTSCH

ENGLISH

JETWING VIL UYANA

Sigiriya, Sri Lanka

VIL UYANA ist eines der ersten Hotels in der Welt, die ein Feuchtgebiet errichtet haben, um ein eigenes Naturreservat zu schaffen. Dieses innovative Konzept bietet einerseits einen Ort für Tiere und Pflanzen, andererseits ermöglicht es Abgeschiedenheit und Ruhe für seine Gäste. Das Ressort hat einen atemberaubenden Ausblick auf den nahe gelegenen Sigiriya Rock, einen fast 200 Meter hohen Felsen, der auch als »achtes Weltwunder« bezeichnet wird.

Die Zimmer des Hotels wurden auf Reisfeldern, in Waldgebieten oder aufgeständert ins Wasser gebaut. Jedes ist großzügig und geschmackvoll gestaltet und bietet ein Höchstmaß an Komfort und Abgeschiedenheit. Die Wasserpavillons sind mit den anderen Gebäuden über Holzstege verbunden und bieten direkten Zugang zu den Booten, mit denen das Reservat erkundet werden kann.

VIL UYANA is one of the first hotels in the world to have built a wetland in order to create its own nature reserve. On the one hand, this innovative concept offers a place for flora and fauna, while on the other, it provides its guests with seclusion and peace. The resort has a breathtaking view of the nearby Sigiriya Rock, just over 650 foot high, which is also described as the »eighth wonder of the world«.

The hotel's rooms were built on rice fields, in woods or set on stilts in the water. Each room is generously and tastefully designed and offers the highest degree of comfort and privacy. The water pavilions are connected with the other buildings via wooden bridges and provide direct access to the boats with which one can explore the nature reserve.

Address
Jetwing Vil Uyana
Sigiriya, Sri Lanka

Website
www.viluyana.com

Speisen kann der Gast in den verschiedenen Restaurants, jedes mit einer speziellen Atmosphäre. Besonderes Ambiente bietet jedoch das intime Dinieren inmitten des Naturreservats. // The guest can enjoy meals in the various restaurants, each with its own special atmosphere, or can experience the particular ambience of intimate dining in the heart of the nature reserve.

Durch großzügige Fensterfronten wird der Blick aus den Bungalows direkt auf die atemberaubende Wasserlandschaft gelenkt. // Thanks to large window façades, the guest's gaze from the bungalows is immediately captivated by the breathtaking waterscape.

DEUTSCH

ENGLISH

HOTEL KAPOK

Beijing, China

IM OSTEN DER VERBOTENEN STADT, nur einen Steinwurf entfernt von den berühmtesten Sehenswürdigkeiten Pekings, steht dieses einzigartige Hotel. Es ist ausgestattet mit 89 Zimmern und Suiten, Restaurants, einer Bar, einer Bibliothek und einem Fitnessraum.

Die semitransparente Fassade ist eine unverwechselbare Mischung aus westlichen Einflüssen und exzellenter chinesischer Architektur. In der Nacht, wenn das Gebäude von innen heraus beleuchtet wird, erscheint es wie eine zeitgemäße Interpretation der traditionellen Laterne. Im Inneren herrscht die gleiche unkonventionelle Verbindung aus Moderne und Tradition. Typisch chinesische Materialien, Möbel und Leuchten finden wie selbstverständlich ihren Platz in dem modern ausgestatteten Haus.

THIS UNIQUE HOTEL is situated in the east of the Forbidden City, only a stone's throw from Beijing's most famous sights. It comprises 89 rooms and suites, restaurants, a bar, a library and a fitness room.

The semi-transparent façade is an unmistakable mixture of western influences and excellent Chinese architecture. At night, when the building is lit from within, the hotel resembles a modern interpretation of the traditional lantern. Inside, the same unconventional fusion of the modern and the traditional dominates. Typical Chinese materials, furniture and lighting all have a natural place in this modern style hotel.

Address
Hotel Kapok
No. 16 Donghuamen Street
Beijing, China

Website
www.hotelkapok.com

Aussicht auf die Verbotene Stadt oder in den beschaulichen Innenhof? – Dieser Frage müssen sich die Gäste der hell eingerichteten Zimmer stellen. // View of the Forbidden City or into a contemplative inner courtyard? A question that guests in the brightly furnished rooms have to answer for themselves.

Das Restaurant befindet sich in der ersten Etage und bietet neben dem Hauptraum noch drei verschiedene private VIP-Räume an. Hier kann zu zweit oder auch mit bis zu 15 Personen gespeist werden. // The restaurant is on the first floor and apart from the main dining room, also offers various private VIP rooms. Try a dinner for two. Alternatively the restaurant caters for groups of up to 15 people.

PH
4
3
2
1
-1
KEATING
1890

DEUTSCH

ENGLISH

KEATING HOTEL

San Diego, USA

IN EINEM 1890 ERBAUTEN Gebäude im Herzen des Gaslamp-Viertels in San Diego entstand ein außergewöhnliches Hotelprojekt: Paolo Pininfarina, bisher bekannt als Designer automobiler Ikonen, hat hier seine einzigartige Handschrift eingebracht. So wird das Innere geprägt durch schnittige Formen, ergonomische Anordnungen und bewährte Materialien aus dem Automobilbau, wie Aluminium und Stahl, und mit der historischen Bausubstanz geschickt verknüpft. Bereits beim Betreten der Lobby wird der eigentliche Designklassiker zelebriert: das Ferrari-Rot. Wände, Decken, Böden und selbst Möbel strahlen geradezu in dieser unverwechselbaren Farbe.

In den Zimmern wurde das Rot dezenter eingesetzt. Weiße Wände, dunkler Holzboden und Möbel setzen die Akzente dennoch gekonnt in Szene. Die Funktionalität, charakteristisch für den Designer, wurde bei den Möbeln bewusst umgesetzt. So befinden sich unter dem Bett herausziehbare Rollkästen, die genügend Stauraum für die Errungenschaften ausgedehnter Shopping-Touren bieten.

AN UNUSUAL HOTEL PROJECT has been developed in a building erected in 1890 in the middle of San Diego's Gaslamp Quarter: Paolo Pininfarina, previously best known as a designer of automobile icons, has introduced his inimitable signature. Thus the interior is characterised by streamlined shapes, ergonomic structures and materials long used in the automotive industry, such as aluminium and steel, and all of this has been cleverly integrated into the historic structure of the building. On entering the lobby, one already sees the real design classic being celebrated: Ferrari red. Walls, ceilings, floors and even the furniture dazzle in this unmistakable colour.

In the rooms, the red is used more discreetly. The highlights are effectively offset however by white walls, dark wooden floors and furniture. The functionality which is characteristic of the designer, was deliberately applied to the furnishings. Thus, beneath the bed one finds a cabinet on rollers, which offers enough space for storing one's trophies after a lengthy shopping trip.

Address
Keating Hotel
432 F st
San Diego, USA

Website
www.thekeating.com

In den Zimmern wurden Teile der Backsteinwände freigelegt, um die historische Bausubstanz erlebbar zu machen. // In the rooms, part of the brick walls have been uncovered, so that the historic structure is immediately apparent.

The Vault – die Weinbar im Herzen des Hotels mit ihren Backsteinwänden und intimem Licht – bietet eine limitierte Pininfarina-Wein-Edition an. // The Vault – the winebar in the middle of the hotel – with its brick walls and intimate lighting offers a limited edition Pininfarina wine.

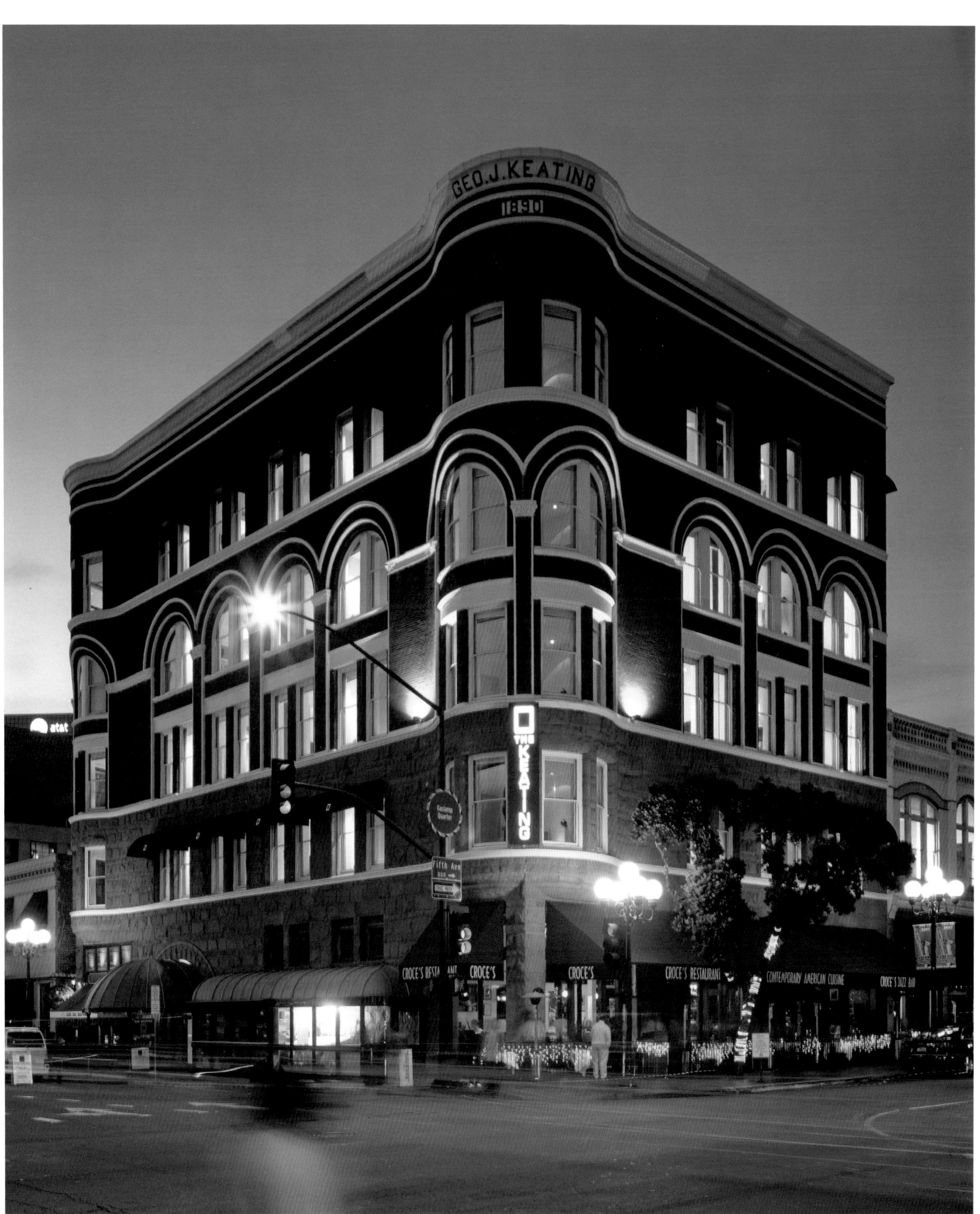
GEO.J.KEATING
1890
THE KEATING
Fifth Ave
CROCE'S RESTAURANT
CROCE'S
CROCE'S
CROCE'S RESTAURANT
CONTEMPORARY AMERICAN CUISINE
CROCE'S JAZZ BAR

DEUTSCH

ENGLISH

LA PURIFICADORA

Puebla, Mexico

IM HISTORISCHEN ZENTRUM von Puebla gelegen, ist dieses umwerfende Hotel aus einer Fabrik des 19. Jahrhunderts hervorgegangen, die einst zur Wasserreinigung und Eisherstellung diente. Diese Tradition von Klarheit und Reinheit ist im La Purificadora nach wie vor spürbar. Bestes Beispiel dafür ist der lang gestreckte, schmale Pool mit gläserner Front auf einer der Terrassen des Hotels. Überhaupt gewähren die vielen Balkone, Terrassen und Treppen spannende Ein- und Ausblicke in und auf das verwinkelte Gebäude.

Die ausschließlich schwarz-weiße Ausstattung der 26 Zimmer ist elegant mit originalen Materialien kombiniert.

THIS STUNNING HOTEL in the historic centre of Puebla was created out of a factory built in the 19th century which was once used for water purification and ice manufacturing. This tradition of clarity and purity is still tangible at La Purificadora. The best example of this is the long, narrow glass-fronted pool on one of the hotel's terraces. The numerous balconies, terraces and stairways offer many an exciting glimpse of this maze of a building.

The 26 rooms are furnished purely in black and white, combining elegantly with the building's original materials.

Address
La Purificadora
Callejón de la
10 Norte 802,
Paseo San Francisco,
Puebla, Mexico

Website
www.lapurificadora.com

In den öffentlichen Räumlichkeiten verbinden sich minimalistisch gestaltete Holzregale mit dem historischen Ambiente zu einem einzigartigen Interieur. // In the public spaces, minimalistically designed wooden shelves merge with the historic ambience to create a unique interior.

Die großzügigen Fensterfronten und die gläsernen Abtrennungen lassen das Licht komplett durch die Zimmer fließen. // The spacious window façades and glass dividers allow light to flood through all the rooms.

Das mexikanische Architekturbüro Legorreta + Legorreta ging behutsam mit der vorhandenen historischen Bausubstanz um. Filigrane Glasbrüstungen wirken fast unsichtbar und rücken damit die alten Gemäuer geschickt in den Vordergrund. // The Mexican architects, Legorreta + Legorreta, were most sensitive in their treatment of the existing historic structure. Filigree glass balustrades are almost invisible, thus cleverly bringing the old walls to the fore.

In der im Innenhof befindlichen Lounge gruppieren sich violette, reduziert gestaltete Sitzmöbel um eine offene Feuerstelle. // The lounge, situated in the inner courtyard, has an open fireplace and is furnished with groups of purple, minimalistically designed seating.

DEUTSCH

ENGLISH

LA RÉSERVE

Paris, France

AM MONUMENTALEN, im Art-déco-Stil gestalteten Place du Trocadéro, mit spektakulärem Blick auf die Stadt und den Eiffelturm, steht dieses einzigartige Pariser Hotel. Die kontrastreiche Farbpalette von Beige bis Schwarz, hohe Wände und Decken sowie riesige, zweiflügelige Fenster lassen die Eleganz der Dreißigerjahre wiederaufleben. Kombiniert wird die historische Bausubstanz mit reduziert gestalteten Designermöbeln namhafter Hersteller. Die zehn Appartements mit ein bis vier Zimmern sind nicht nur für kurze Städtetrips ausgelegt, sondern bieten auch die Möglichkeit zu längeren Aufenthalten.

THIS UNIQUE PARIS HOTEL is located at the monumental Art Deco Place du Trocadéro, with a spectacular view of the city and the Eiffel Tower. The broad contrast of colours from beige to black, high walls and ceilings and enormous, double-winged windows recreate the elegance of the 1930s. The historic structure is combined with the minimalist furniture of well known designers. The ten apartments, with one to four rooms, are designed not only for short visits to the city but are also suitable for longer stays.

Address
La Réserve
10 Place du Trocadéro
Paris, France

Website
www.lareserve-paris.com

Das herrschaftliche Eckhaus im 16. Arrondissement zieht die Blicke der Passanten auf sich. // This magnificent corner house in the 16th arrondissement always attracts the attention of those passing by.

Modern interpretierte Himmelbetten und zeitgemäße Badezimmermöbel werden mit prachtvollen Einzelstücken geschickt kombiniert. // Modernly interpreted four poster beds and contemporary bathroom furnishings are cleverly combined with ornate one-off pieces.

CHANEL

DEUTSCH

LABRIZ SILHOUETTE

Seychelles

DAS RESORT LABRIZ liegt auf einer traumhaften Seychellen-Insel. Sie ist nur etwa 17 Kilometer von der Hauptinsel Mahé entfernt und besonders für Naturliebhaber und Wanderer empfehlenswert. Mit dem Boot dauert die Überfahrt etwa 45 Minuten, mit dem Helikopter sind es etwa 15 Minuten.

Mehrere ausgedehnte Wanderpfade verlaufen über die Insel und führen bis auf den höchsten Berg und an der wilden Küste entlang. Hier findet man ein Naturreservat für eine seltene Gattung von Riesenschildkröten. Insbesondere für Wasserliebhaber hat die Anlage einiges zu bieten: In der durch ein Riff geschützten Lagune befinden sich traumhafte Tauch- und Schnorchelgebiete. Das Leben auf Silhouette Island spielte sich eigentlich bis vor Kurzem noch wie vor hundert Jahren ab. Es ist also genau der richtige Platz zum Entspannen.

Das Labriz, direkt an einem traumhaften Sandstrand gelegen, eingerahmt von Palmen, verfügt über 110 Villen und Pavillons. Die moderne Einrichtung wird durch traditionelle Elemente akzentuiert. Großzügige Badezimmer komplettieren die luxuriöse Ausstattung. In den 17 Pavillons öffnet sich das Bad zu einem privaten Garten mit Pool und Regendusche.

ENGLISH

THE LABRIZ RESORT is located on a heavenly island in the Seychelles. It is only around ten miles from the largest island, Mahé, and is highly recommended for nature lovers and walkers. The crossing takes about 45 minutes by boat, or 15 by helicopter.

Several extensive walking tracks criss-cross the island, leading to the highest mountain and along the wild coastline. On the island there is a nature reserve for a rare species of giant tortoise. The resort is of particular interest to water lovers: in the lagoon, which is protected by a reef, there are superb diving and snorkelling areas. Until recently, the way of life at Silhouette had hardly changed in a century, making it the ideal place for relaxing.

The Labriz, set directly on a gorgeous sandy beach and framed by palms, has over 100 villas and pavilions. The modern furnishings are accented with traditional elements. Spacious bathrooms complete the luxurious appointments. In the 17 pavilions, the bathroom opens up into a private garden with pool and rain shower.

Address
Labriz Silhouette
Silhouette Island,
Seychelles

Website
www.labriz-seychelles.com

Die Gäste treten von ihren Bungalows durch einen schmalen Palmen-Streifen direkt an den weißen Sandstrand. // Guests enter their bungalows through a small strip of palms, directly on the white sandy beach.

Der mit kleinen türkisfarbenen Mosaikfliesen gestaltete Pool ist direkt vom Zimmer aus erreichbar und bietet einen atemberaubenden Blick auf die umgebende Landschaft. // The pool, decorated with small turquoise mosaic tiles can be reached directly from the room and offers a breathtaking view of the surrounding landscape.

DEUTSCH

ENGLISH

LÁNCHÍD 19

Budapest, Hungary

BENANNT NACH der berühmten Kettenbrücke (»lánchíd« bedeutet Brücke) Budapests, ist dieses Hotel ein besonderes Highlight in dem von Häusern aus dem 19. Jahrhundert dominierten Viertel. Das Team aus Architekten und Designern kreierte eine bewegliche, einem Akkordeon ähnliche Glasfassade, die mithilfe eines ausgeklügelten Lichtsystems ständig die Farbe wechselt. Auch im Inneren spielt Glas eine wichtige Rolle: Ein gebäudehohes Atrium aus Glas über der Lobby flutet die öffentlichen Räume und die Zugänge zu den Gästezimmern mit Tageslicht. Und der gläserne Boden der Lobby öffnet den Blick auf die darunter liegenden römischen Ruinen.

In den hellen, in kühlen Farben gehaltenen Zimmern erlauben Glasbrüstungen an den Balkonen und raumhohe Fensterscheiben immer wieder interessante Ausblicke auf die Donau, die Brücke und die Stadt. Designklassiker von Alvar Aalto werden geschickt mit maßgefertigten Möbeln kombiniert.

NAMED AFTER Budapest's famous chain bridges (»lánchíd« means bridge), the hotel is a special highlight in this district, dominated by 19th century houses. The team of architects and designers has created a mobile glass façade, resembling an accordion, which continually changes colour thanks to an ingenious lighting system. Inside too, glass plays an important role: an atrium the height of the entire building floods the public spaces and entrances to the guest rooms with daylight. The lobby's glass floor offers a view of the Roman ruins lying below.

In the rooms, which are bright and decorated in cool colours, glass balustrades on the balconies and floor to ceiling windows afford the guest many interesting views of the Danube, the bridge and the city. Design classics by Alvar Aalto are cleverly combined with custom furniture.

Address
Lánchíd 19
Lánchíd utca 19-21
Budapest, Hungary

Website
www.lanchid19hotel.hu

Die mit kleinen LEDs beleuchteten Spiegel reflektieren die exquisit eingerichteten schwarz-weißen Badezimmer. // The mirrors, lit with small LEDs, reflect the exquisitely furnished, black and white bathrooms.

Von der Badewanne kann der Gast den Blick durch die gläsernen Wände hindurch über Terrasse und Donau bis hin zur Burg schweifen lassen. // From the bathtub, the guest can let his gaze wander through the terrace's glass walls to the Danube and the castle.

DEUTSCH

ENGLISH

LOVE HOTEL

Design Concept

»EIN ORT, DER DIE LIEBE ZELEBRIERT.« So beschreiben die Designer des Love Hotels ihr Konzept. Hier soll der Gast sich in angemessener Umgebung mit seinem Partner zurückziehen und vor den Blicken der Außenwelt geschützt intim sein können. Schon die Lobby symbolisiert das Werben um den Partner: Zitate zu Liebe und Leidenschaft sind in goldenen Mosaiksteinchen auf die rote Wand geschrieben. Die Zimmer präsentieren sich in sündigem Rot, gepaart mit unschuldigem Weiß. Videoprojektionen an den Wänden erzeugen verschiedene Szenarien, wie etwa Aufregung oder Entspannung. Organische Formen, eine großzügige Badewanne und ein ebensolches Bett beflügeln die Fantasie. An einer Wand verbergen sich hinter Schiebetüren verschiedene Räume, wie Ankleidezimmer und Bäder.

»A PLACE THAT CELEBRATES LOVE«, is how the designers of the Love Hotel describe their concept. Here, the guest should be able to withdraw with his partner to the right surroundings and enjoy moments of intimacy, protected from the gaze of the outside world. The lobby itself makes many references to wooing a partner: quotations about love and passion are written on the red wall in golden mosaic tiles. The rooms are decorated in sinful red, coupled with innocent white. Video projections on the walls create various scenarios, such as excitement or relaxation. Organic shapes, a generously-sized bathtub and an equally large bed lend wings to the imagination. Various rooms, such as dressing rooms and bathrooms are concealed along one wall behind sliding doors.

Love Hotel
Concept

Website
www.studio63.it

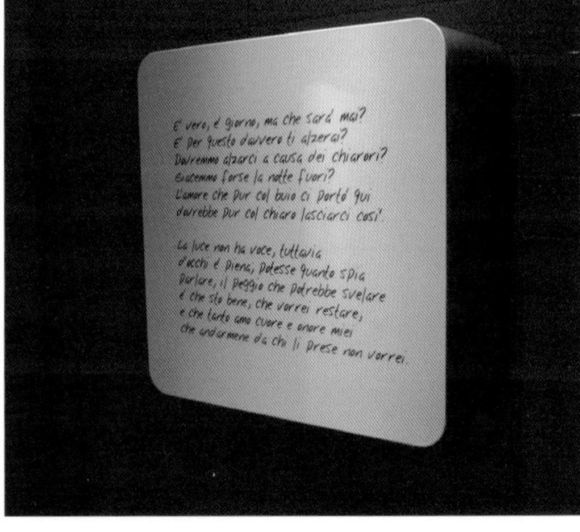
E' vero, è giorno, ma che sarà mai?
E per questo davvero ti alzerai?
Dovremmo alzarci a causa dei chiarori?
Giacemmo forse la notte fuori?
L'amore che pur col buio ci portò qui
dovrebbe pur col chiaro lasciarci così.
La luce non ha voce, tuttavia
d'occhi è piena, potesse quanto spia
parlare, il peggio che potrebbe svelare
è che sto bene, che vorrei restare,
e che tanto amo cuore e onore miei
che andarmene da chi li prese non vorrei.

Der Gast findet immer wieder Zitate aus Literatur und Poesie – auch an ungewöhnlichen Orten, wie zum Beispiel auf Leuchtkörpern. // The guest repeatedly encounters lines of literature or poetry, even in unusual places, such as on lighting.

Auch im Ankleidezimmer spielen die Designer mit den Insignien des Erotischen: An langen Silberketten hängt die Kleidung von der Decke. // In the dressing room too, the designers have been inspired by erotic insignia: clothing hangs from the ceiling on long silver chains …

DEUTSCH

ENGLISH

MARQUÉS DE RISCAL

Elciego, Spain

IM HERZEN der berühmten spanischen Weinregion Rioja, in der mittelalterlichen Stadt Elciego, vereint sich traditionelle Weinkultur mit avantgardistischer Architektur. Das Hotel mit seinen geschwungenen Wänden und einem Dach aus glänzendem Titan bildet einen spektakulären Kontrast zu den historischen Weinkellern von 1858. Jedes der 43 luxuriösen Zimmer hat eine andere Form, eine andere Ausrichtung. Das Interieur ist charakteristisch für Frank O. Gehrys avantgardistisches Design: Leder und grobes Walnussholz in den Zimmern sowie dunkler Marmor in den Bädern harmonieren perfekt mit Möbelstücken des Architekten und einiger seiner berühmten Kollegen wie Alvar Aalto. Das Kaminzimmer mit hauseigener Bibliothek lädt ein zu Weinproben in angemessenem Ambiente.

IN THE HEART of the famous Spanish wine region of Rioja, in the medieval town of Elciego, traditional viniculture meets avant garde architecture. With its curved walls and sparkling titanium roof, the hotel forms a spectacular contrast to the historic wine cellars built in 1858. Each of the 43 luxuriously appointed rooms is differently shaped and decorated. The interior is typical of Frank O. Gehry's avant garde design: leather and rough walnut wood in the rooms and dark marble in the bathrooms harmonise perfectly with the architect's furniture and that of some of his famous colleagues, such as Alvar Aalto. The fireplace room with its own library offers the perfect ambience for a wine tasting.

Address
Marqués de Riscal
Calle Torrea, 1
Elciego, Spain

Website
www.starwoodhotels.com

Inmitten der sanften Weinhügel zeigt sich das Hotel in seiner ganzen Pracht. Die Titanbänder reflektieren die Farben und das Licht der einzigartigen Landschaft. //
The hotel, set in the middle of a gentle wine mountain, reveals itself in all its glory. The titanium ribbons reflect the colours and the light of this unique landscape.

Gläserne Gänge zwischen dem historischen Gebäudeteil und dem Gehry-Flügel erlauben immer wieder Blicke auf die außergewöhnliche Architektur. // Glass walkways between the historic parts of the building and the Gehry Wing give the guest many opportunities to take in the unusual architecture.

In den Kellern des Hotels lagern die weltberühmten Weine des spanischen Traditionsunternehmens Herederos del Marqués de Riscal. // The world famous wines from the traditional wine estate, Herederos del Marqués de Riscal, are laid down in the hotel's cellars.

Die beiden Restaurants bieten eine ausgezeichnete Auswahl an Weinen aus der ganzen Welt sowie traditionelle baskisch-riojanische Küche, kombiniert mit modernen Einflüssen. // The two restaurants offer an excellent choice of wines from all over the world, as well as traditional Basque-Riojan cuisine, combined with modern influences.

Die Lounge und die Bibliothek auf dem Dach des Hotels sorgen für eine stilvolle und gleichzeitig gemütliche Atmosphäre bei einzigartigem Panoramablick. // The lounge and library on the roof of the hotel offer a stylish yet comfortable atmosphere with a unique panorama view.

Das Caudalíe Vinothérapie® Spa bildet das Zentrum der Freizeiteinrichtungen mit einem Innenpool, einem Fitness-Center, einem Whirlpool, einer erfrischenden Dusche und 14 Behandlungsräumen für verschiedene »Weintherapie«-Massagen und -Behandlungen. Alle Produkte sind aus Traubenextrakt und Wasser hergestellt und wurden exklusiv entwickelt. // The Caudalíe Vinothéraphie® Spa lies at the heart of the recreational amenities, with an indoor pool, a fitness centre, a whirlpool, a refreshing shower and 14 treatment rooms for various »wine therapy« massages and treatments. All products are produced from grape extract and water and are exclusively developed.

DEUTSCH

ENGLISH

MÖVENPICK RESORT & SPA MAURITIUS

Bel Ombre, Mauritius

AN DER SÜDWESTKÜSTE von Mauritius gelegen, eingebettet in die unberührte Natur von Bel Ombre, befindet sich das Mövenpick Resort & Spa. Schon der Eingangsbereich mit seinem großzügigen Raumangebot und dem Durchblick zur nahen Lagune stimmt den Gast auf die Schönheit der Anlage ein. Die Gebäude verteilen sich in dem über sieben Hektar großen tropischen Garten mit exotischen Pflanzen und Früchten. Zum Resort gehört ein 500 Meter langer Privatstrand mit verstreuten Sonnenliegen aus Teakholz und Sonnenschirmen aus Palmenzweigen.

Alle Zimmer, Suiten und auch die Villa sind zum Ozean orientiert. Die Räumlichkeiten sind komfortabel und lichtdurchflutet, dank der großen Fenster in den Schlafräumen und Badezimmern, die das Licht von beiden Seiten auffangen.

THE MÖVENPICK RESORT & SPA is situated on the south west coast of Mauritius, embedded in the unspoilt nature of Bel Ombre. The entrance area, with its generous space and view through to the nearby lagoon, primes the guest for the beauty of the resort. The buildings are spread out over the 17 acre tropical garden with its exotic plants and fruit. The resort also has a private beach, nearly a mile long on which teak loungers and palm leaf sunshades are scattered.

All of the rooms, suites and the villa face the ocean. The accommodation is comfortable, with plenty of light thanks to the large windows in the bedrooms and bathrooms which catch the light from both sides.

Address
Mövenpick Resort & Spa Mauritius
Allee des Cocotiers
Bel Ombre, Mauritius

Website
www.moevenpick-hotels.com

Die Gäste haben die Möglichkeit, am Strand zu speisen oder auch unter dem Sternenhimmel, geschützt durch ein Palmendach. //
Guests can dine on the beach or beneath the stars, protected by a palm canopy.

DEUTSCH

ENGLISH

MILLENNIUM HILTON BANGKOK

Bangkok, Thailand

ÜBER DEM FLUSS CHAO PRAYA thronend, bietet das Millennium Hilton Bangkok einen herrlichen Blick auf die Stadt.

Das Fünf-Sterne-Haus in Bangkoks Innenstadt verfügt über einen erstklassigen Service. Dazu gehört auch der kostenlose Shuttle-Service zur Sky-Bahn-Station Saphan Taksin und zum Shopping-Komplex River City.

Schon die Lobby besticht durch ihre prachtvolle, glamouröse Ausstattung. Glänzende Böden, edle Materialien und funkelnde Lüster lassen ein Erlebnis der Extraklasse erahnen. Fünf Bars und Cafés sowie drei Restaurants entführen den Gast in einzigartige Kulissen.

ENTHRONED ABOVE the Chao Praya River, the Millennium Hilton Bangkok offers a fabulous view of the city.

This five star hotel in the heart of Bangkok provides first class service, including a free shuttle to the Saphan Taksin Sky Rail station and to the River City shopping complex. The guest will be impressed on merely stepping into the sumptuous and glamorous lobby. Sparkling floors, luxurious materials and glittering lights give that extra touch of class. Each of the five bars and cafés, as well as three restaurants, carry the guest off into an unique setting.

Address
Millennium Hilton Bangkok
123 Charoennakorn Road
Bangkok, Thailand

Website
www.hilton.com

Das erste Highlight ist in der 32. Etage des Hochhauses untergebracht: das Three Sixty in romantischem Ambiente, mit sanfterJazzmusik und erlesenen Cocktails. Hier beeindruckt ein überwältigender Blick von der rotierenden Hotelbar auf die Stadt. // The first highlight is the romantic Three Sixty on the 32nd floor of the skyscraper, with quiet jazz music and excellent cocktails. Here one is overwhelmed by the view of the city from the rotating hotel bar.

Sonne, weißen Sand und Cocktailspezialitäten bietet die Bar The Beach. Entspannung auf einem der Liegestühle am Pool im 4. Geschoss ist garantiert. Frisch gepresste Säfte und Fruchtshakes oder Snacks runden das Strandfeeling perfekt ab. // Sun, white sand and cocktail specialities are on offer at The Beach bar. Relaxation is guaranteed in a lounger beside the pool on the 4th floor. Freshly squeezed juices and fruit shakes or snacks give one that perfect beach feeling.

Exklusive Materialien, dezente Grundfarben, stimmungsvolle Beleuchtung und rote Farbakzente verleihen der Lobby einen einzigartigen Glanz. // Exclusive materials, restrained basic colours, atmospheric lighting and red highlights lend the lobby a unique glamour.

Atrien über mehrere Geschosse, Galerien und transparente Glaselemente erschaffen großzügige Aus- und Einblicke. // Atria extending over several floors, galleries and transparent glass elements create plenty of room for views – of both inside and outside the hotel.

Gedämpftes Licht, Ledersofas und eine beleuchtete Theke bestimmen das Ambiente des Zeta. Mit ihrem preisgekrönten Londoner Bar-Design, der anregenden Musik und den Champagnercocktails lädt die Bar zum Tanzen bis in die frühen Morgenstunden ein. // Subdued lighting, leather couches and an illuminated bar define the atmosphere in Zeta. This bar, with its prize-winning London bar design, stimulating music and champagne cocktails is just the place to dance until the small hours.

Ein besonderer Zufluchtsort ist das hauseigene Spa: In den zehn Behandlungsräumen wird der Gast mit allen Annehmlichkeiten verwöhnt. // The perfect retreat is the in-house spa: the guest can enjoy being pampered in every way in ten different treatment rooms.

In den Zimmern herrscht ein exklusives und mondänes Ambiente: Dunkles Holz und helle Stoffe harmonieren mit den reduziert gestalteten Möbeln. // An exclusive and sophisticated ambience dominates in the rooms. Dark wood and light textiles harmonise with the minimalist furniture.

DEUTSCH

ENGLISH

ONE WORLD HOTEL

Selangor, Malaysia

FÜNFZEHN MINUTEN von der Innenstadt Kuala Lumpurs entfernt, hat das Fünf-Sterne-Haus One World Hotel seine Pforten geöffnet. Das imposante Gebäude steht in einem modernen, repräsentativen Wohngebiet und ist auf Business-Reisende ebenso wie auf den individuellen Erholungs- und Kultururlauber ausgerichtet.

Das Hotel besticht durch seinen prunkvollen klassisch-eleganten Stil, der sich schon in der Lobby zeigt und in den anderen Räumlichkeiten wieder aufgenommen wird. In den 438 Zimmern und Suiten wurde bei der Einrichtung auf Innovation, Bequemlichkeit und Raffinesse Wert gelegt. Warme, einladende, sanfte Farbschattierungen in Beige und Braun, knisternde weiße Laken, edle Bettwäsche und reich verzierte Wände erzeugen in den Zimmern ein sinnliches Ambiente. Ausgesuchte Kunstobjekte und zeitgemäße Dekorationen spiegeln den modernen Geist der asiatischen Metropole wider. Auch in den Badezimmern herrscht Luxus pur: Separate Duschen und Wannen gehören ebenso selbstverständlich zur Ausstattung wie persönliche Handtücher, Bademäntel oder Hausschuhe.

THE FIVE STAR ONE WORLD HOTEL has opened its doors fifteen minutes from the centre of Kuala Lumpur. This impressive building is located in a modern and prestigious residential area and is designed both for business travellers and for individual holidaymakers and cultural tourists.

The hotel's grand, classically elegant style, which is immediately apparent in the lobby and carries through to the other rooms, is most attractive. In furnishing the 438 rooms and suites, the keywords were innovation, comfort and refinement. Soft, warm and inviting shades of beige and brown, crisp white sheets, fine bed linen and richly ornamented walls create a sensual ambience in the rooms. Selected works of art and contemporary decoration reflect the modern spirit of this Asian metropolis. In the bathrooms too, the guest can enjoy pure luxury: separate showers and bathtubs are standard, as are personal hand towels, bathrobes and slippers.

Address
One World Hotel
First Avenue
Petaling Jaya, Selangor
Malaysia

Website
www.oneworldhotel.com.my

Glänzende Marmorböden und prächtige Kronleuchter empfangen den Gast in der Lobby und lassen den zu erwartenden Luxus erahnen. // Polished marble floors and a magnificent chandelier welcome the guest in the lobby and hint at the luxury which awaits.

DEUTSCH

ENGLISH

MOHR LIFE RESORT

Lermoos, Austria

AM FUSSE DER ZUGSPITZE, vor der atemberaubenden Kulisse der Tiroler Alpen, liegt dieses einzigartige Wellnesshotel. Das denkmalgeschützte, 200 Jahre alte Stammhaus wurde nun durch einen modernen Anbau ergänzt. Hier stehen Urlaubsfreude und Vergnügen im Mittelpunkt, genauso wie höchstes Wohlbefinden und vollkommener Genuss. Die architektonischen Gegensätze ergeben ein innovatives Hoteldesign und ein intensives Lebensgefühl. Überall im Resort finden sich die Elemente Feuer, Wasser, Stein wieder, kombiniert mit zeitgemäßem Design und modernen Materialien.

Um das Gefühl von Erholung und Wohlbefinden spürbar zu machen, wurde bei der Zimmereinrichtung größter Wert auf eine exklusive Ausstattung gelegt. So ist in vielen Räumen Zirbenholz verwendet worden, ein Material, dem seit Jahrhunderten positive Eigenschaften für bessere Schlaf- und Erholungsqualität zugesprochen werden. Die Ausstattung ist extravagant und stylisch. Durch den Umbau neu hinzugekommen sind weitere 19 moderne Zirben-Zimmer und »Kuschelsuiten«. Traumhaft schön gestaltet und äußerst großzügig, bietet die »Mega-Suite« mit 100 Quadratmetern Wohnfläche, Sauna, Panoramawanne sowie einer Terrasse mit fantastischem Ausblick ein besonderes Wohlfühlerlebnis.

THIS UNIQUE WELLNESS HOTEL is set at the foot of the Zugspitze Mountain, in front of the breathtaking scenery of the Tyrolean Alps. The main building, which is 200 years old and listed, has been extended with a modern annex. This is a place where holiday pleasure and enjoyment are centre stage, as are absolute wellbeing and consummate indulgence. The architectural contrasts have created an innovative hotel design and an intensely positive sense of life. The elements of fire, water and stone are encountered repeatedly throughout the hotel, combined with contemporary design and modern materials.

In order to make the sense of recovery and wellbeing tangible, the greatest of care has been taken to ensure the exclusive furnishing of the rooms. Thus many of the rooms are fitted with stone pine, which for centuries has been ascribed the power to improve sleep and aid recuperation. The furnishings are extravagant and stylish. Thanks to the conversion, there are an additional 19 modern stone pine rooms and romantic suites for two. Beautifully designed and extremely spacious, the Mega Suite is a very special experience with a living space of 1,077 square feet and including sauna, panorama tub and a terrace with a fantastic view.

Address
Mohr Life Resort
Innsbruckerstrasse 40
Lermoos, Austria

Website
www.mohr-life-resort.at

In der Lobby trifft Geschichte auf zeitgemäßes Design: Einbauten aus traditionellen Holzarten werden mit modernen Materialien und leuchtenden Farben kombiniert. // In the lobby, history meets contemporary design. Fittings made with traditional timbers are combined with modern materials and brilliant colours.

Zwei Fackeln beleuchten den Weg zum Hotel und werden vom goldenen Eingangsportal reflektiert. // Two torches light the way to the hotel and are reflected in the golden entrance portal.

So genannte Vogelnester dienen zum Entspannen und Relaxen und bieten neben der angenehmen Lichtatmosphäre auch einen beeindruckenden Ausblick auf die Zugspitze. // So called birds' nests provide relaxation and, apart from the pleasing light, also offer an impressive view of the Zugspitze.

Die Gäste des Wellnesshotels können sich an den vielen »Feuerstellen« wärmen und dabei genussvoll einen Drink zu sich nehmen. // Guests at the wellness hotel can warm up at one of many »fireplaces« and enjoy a drink at the same time.

Das 17 Meter lange Panorama-Hallenbad bietet einen grandiosen Ausblick über die verträumte Mooslandschaft und zur Zugspitze. Die Front des Poolbereichs besteht aus einer großflächigen Glasfassade und ist in RGB-Licht (Rot, Grün, Blau) getaucht. Über dem Pool schweben die Vogelnester, die zum Relaxen einladen. // The panorama indoor pool measures almost 56 feet and provides a marvellous view of the enchanting moss landscape and the Zugspitze. The front of the pool area comprises a large glass façade which is bathed in RGB (red, green, blue) light. The birds' nests float above the pool, inviting the guest to relax.

Vom heißen Sole-Außenbecken aus hat der Gast einen atemberaubenden Blick auf die unberührte Natur und die Tiroler Berge. // From the hot outdoor brine pool, the guest has a breath-taking view of unspoilt nature and the Tyrol mountains.

DEUTSCH

ENGLISH

POD HOTEL

New York City, USA

UNTERGEBRACHT IN EINEM in den Zwanzigerjahren erbauten Gebäude im Herzen Manhattans ist das neu gestaltete und umgebaute Pod Hotel. Der Name ist Programm: Wie Schoten sind die 347 Zimmer dicht an dicht gereiht in dem imposanten Gebäude. Zugrunde liegt das Konzept, hochwertige Ausstattung und moderne Technologie zu moderaten Preisen anzubieten. Die Zielgruppe sind stylische Großstadtbesucher, die ihr Geld und ihre Zeit lieber in die Erkundung der Stadt als in teure Hotelzimmer stecken. Das Design ist eine Mischung aus ausgeklügelten Raumkonzepten, einfallsreichen Gestaltungsideen und der Ästhetik von Design-Ikonen wie Charles und Ray Eames.

Bei der Ausstattung der Hotelzimmer ließ sich die Designerin Vanessa Guilford von den platzsparenden Raumkonzepten in Zügen, Flugzeugen oder Booten inspirieren. So sind die Zimmer wahre Platz-Wunder: Wandschränke, Schubkästen unter den Betten oder multifunktionale Tisch- und Stuhlkombinationen bieten genug Raum für die Habseligkeiten der Gäste. Die moderne und skurril anmutende Einrichtung der Lobby wird von einer Auswahl ungewöhnlicher Materialien und Texturen dominiert. Ein hellgrüner, beleuchteter Tresen heißt den Besucher willkommen.

HOUSED IN A BUILDING erected in the 1920s in the heart of Manhattan, is the converted and newly designed Pod Hotel. The name also explains the design: the 347 rooms are lined up closely beside each other in this imposing building, like peas in a pod. The underlying concept is to offer high quality furnishing and modern technology at reasonable prices. The hotel's target group are stylish urban tourists, who prefer to spend their time and money on exploring their surroundings, than on an expensive hotel room. The design is a mix of ingenious room concepts, inventive design ideas and the aesthetic of design icons such as Charles and Ray Eames.

In furnishing the rooms, the designer, Vanessa Guilford, was inspired by space-saving concepts such as those used in trains, planes and boats. This means the rooms are truly miraculous in their use of space: built-in cupboards, rolling cabinets under the beds and multifunctional table and chair combinations ensure plenty of room for the guest's personal items. The modern and whimsical design of the lobby is dominated by the choice of unusual materials and textures. The reception desk is a light green, illuminated counter.

Address
The Pod Hotel
230 East 51st St
New York City, USA

Website
www.thepodhotel.com

Geschickt wird die reduzierte Grundausstattung mit Stoffen von Charles und Ray Eames sowie Reproduktionen ihrer Stühle kombiniert. // The minimalised basic fitout is cleverly combined with Charles and Ray Eames' textiles and reproductions of their chairs.

DEUTSCH

ENGLISH

PORTO PALÁCIO

Porto, Portugal

NACH SEINER KOMPLETTRENOVIERUNG im Jahr 2006 erstrahlt das Hotel heute in neuem Glanz. Die Zimmer wurden dabei in zwei Kategorien unterteilt: Executive und Deluxe. Möbel und Materialien wurden in unterschiedlicher Weise gestaltet und geben damit den beiden Zimmerarten jeweils einen eigenen Charakter. In den öffentlichen Räumen wurde besonderer Wert auf Licht, Akustik und neueste Technologie gelegt.

Die Ecken der Gästezimmer wurden abgerundet und geben, mit den ebenfalls abgerundeten Möbeln, dem Design der Räume einen eleganten Art-déco-Touch. Um in allen Bereichen des Zimmers Tageslicht zu gewährleisten, wurden verspiegelte Schiebetüren und großflächige, semitransparente Glasfenster zwischen Badezimmer, Ankleide und Schlafzimmer eingesetzt. Durch diese Maßnahmen eröffnet sich dem Gast ein großzügig wirkendes Zimmer mit ausreichend Licht in allen Bereichen.

FOLLOWING ITS COMPLETE RENOVATION in 2006 the hotel is now restored in all its glory. The rooms have been divided into two categories – Executive and Deluxe. Furniture and materials have been designed in different ways giving the two types of room their own character. In the public spaces special emphasis has been placed on light, acoustics and the latest technology.

The corners of the guest rooms have been rounded and, together with the equally rounded furniture, give the design of the rooms an elegant Art Deco touch. To ensure daylight in all areas of the room, mirrored sliding doors and large, semi-transparent panes of glass between bathroom, dressing area and bedroom have been installed. Thanks to these, the rooms appear very spacious and full of light in every corner.

Address
Hotel Porto Palácio
Av. Boavista, 1269
Porto, Portugal

Website
www.hotelportopalacio.com

Dezente Grautöne in allen Schattierungen, edle Materialien und gekonnt eingesetzte indirekte Lichtquellen verleihen den Hotelzimmern ein exquisites und luxuriöses Ambiente. // Muted grey in every possible shade, costly materials and cleverly placed indirect lighting give the hotel rooms an exquisite and luxurious ambience.

DEUTSCH

ENGLISH

PARK HOTEL MUMBAI

Mumbai, India

DAS PARK HOTEL liegt inmitten des zentralen Geschäftszentrums Belapur der indischen Metropole Mumbai und ermöglicht zugleich atemberaubende Ausblicke auf die umliegenden grünen Hügel. Für Business- wie für Freizeit-Reisende bietet das Hotel eine zeitgemäße und elegante Kulisse. Im Interieur verschmelzen Ost und West, modernste Technologie und lokales Handwerk. Traditionelle indische Muster und Textilien werden geschmackvoll mit klaren Linien und modernem Design kombiniert.

Als eine Hommage an die Moderne und an Le Corbusier wurde das Hotel mit offenen Räumen und fließenden Übergängen zwischen den verschiedenen Teilen des Hauses geplant. Strahlendes Weiß beherrscht nicht nur die Fassade des Fünfsternehotels, sondern auch den Innenhof, um den sich die 80 Zimmer gruppieren.

THE PARK HOTEL is in the heart of the main Belapur business centre in the Indian city of Mumbai and offers breathtaking views of the surrounding green hills. Ideal both for business travellers and holiday visitors, the hotel is contemporary and elegant. Inside, east and west fuse with cutting edge technology and local handicraft. Traditional Indian patterns and textiles are tastefully combined with clean lines and modern design.

As a hommage to Modernism and Le Corbusier, the hotel was planned with open spaces and flowing passageways between the different parts of the building. Dazzling white dominates not only on the façade of this five star hotel, but also in the inner courtyard around which the 80 rooms are grouped.

Address
Park Hotel Mumbai
No 1, Sector 10, CBD
Belapur
Navi Mumbai, India

Website
navimumbai.
theparkhotels.com

Das Bamboo ist eines von vier Restaurants. Es bietet seinen Gästen traditionelle chinesische Küche in einem ungewöhnlichen Ambiente. Weißer Marmor und horizontal verkleidete Eichenpfeiler bieten einen spannenden Kontrast zu den grünen Wänden und den im gleichen Farbton gepolsterten Stühlen. // The Bamboo is one of four restaurants and offers its guests traditional Chinese cuisine in an unusual atmosphere. White marble and horizontally panelled oak pillars offer an exciting contrast to the green walls and the chairs, upholstered in the same colour.

DEUTSCH

ENGLISH

RADISSON HOTEL PUDONG CENTURY PARK

Shanghai, China

ZEITGEMÄSSES DESIGN, speziell für dieses Projekt in Auftrag gegebene Kunstobjekte und traditionell-chinesisch inspirierte Gebrauchsgegenstände verbinden sich in diesem Hotel zu einem harmonischen Ganzen. Die Zimmer sind bewusst zurückhaltend und minimalistisch gestaltet, um einladend und beruhigend auf den Gast zu wirken. Große Fenster, die vom Boden bis zur Decke reichen, lassen viel natürliches Licht herein und unterstreichen die Helligkeit der vorwiegend weißen Möblierung. Vereinzelte Farbmomente akzentuieren ungewöhnliche Stellen, wie beispielsweise eine Grafik des Künstlers Wang Xiao Hui, die an der Badezimmerdecke sowie am Kopfende des Betts erscheint.

CONTEMPORARY DESIGN, specially commissioned works of art and items for daily use inspired by Chinese tradition are blended in this hotel to create a harmonious whole. The rooms are deliberately restrained and minimalist, so that they are more inviting and calming for the guest. Large, floor to ceiling windows allow in plenty of natural light and underline the brightness of the predominantly white furnishings. Individual spots of colour are used for highlighting in unusual places, such as a graphic by the artist, Wang Xiao Hui, placed on the bathroom ceiling and at the head of the bed.

Address
Radisson Hotel Pudong Century Park
Ying Chun Road
Pudong, Shanghai, China

Website
www.radisson.com

Das chinesische Restaurant Yar Chi Ting befindet sich im dritten Geschoss des Hotels und beeindruckt durch sein außergewöhnliches Interieur: Riesige Kandelaber, Deckenleuchten, die Essstäbchen darstellen, rechteckige Tische sowie rot gepolsterte Bänke und Hocker verbinden traditionelle Elemente mit modernem Design. // The Chinese restaurant, Yar Chi Ting, is on the third floor of the hotel and its unusual interior is striking. Enormous candelabra, ceiling lights representing chopsticks, rectangular tables and red-upholstered benches and stools combine traditional elements with modern design.

Angrenzend an die Lobby befindet sich eine Lounge, die sich als Treffpunkt wie auch für kleine Pausen eignet. Gestaltet wurde sie mit einer Kombination aus Kristallperlenvorhängen und zeitgemäßen Möbeln. // Adjacent to the lobby there is a lounge which is ideal as a meeting place or for a short break. It has been designed using a combination of crystal bead curtains and contemporary furniture.

Um ein zurückhaltendes Ambiente zu schaffen, wurden für die Zimmer Möbel und Ausstattungen in hellem Weiß gewählt, kombiniert mit Grau und Akzenten in Apfelgrün. // To create a subdued ambience in the guest rooms, furnishings are in bright white, combined with grey and apple green highlights.

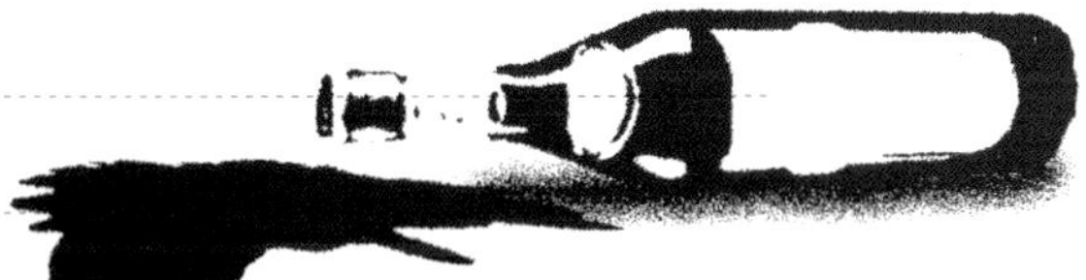

DEUTSCH

ENGLISH

RIAD MERIEM

Riad, Morocco

IN DER MEDINA, dem ältesten Quartier von Marrakesch, prägen enge Gassen, orientalische Häuser und Stadtpaläste das Bild und in der Luft liegt der Duft exotischer Gewürze. Die Zeit scheint stehengeblieben zu sein. Hier, inmitten des geschäftigen Treibens auf den Straßen, steht das Hotel Riad Meriem. Dieses kleine, aber feine Haus wurde mit viel Liebe zur arabischen Kultur und Kunst ausgestattet. Der New Yorker Designer Thomas Hays kreierte ein sinnliches Ambiente aus orientalischen Stoffen, erlesenen Gemälden und seinen eigenen, kunstvollen Fotografien. Um die Authentizität zu wahren, wurden die Arbeiten am Hotel und an der Einrichtung ausschließlich von arabischen Handwerkern in Handarbeit ausgeführt.

Jeder der Namen der fünf individuell gestalteten Zimmer verweist auf ihr jeweiliges Konzept: In der Star Suite hängen leuchtende Sterne von der Decke, während großflächige Matisse-Drucke die gleichnamige Suite schmücken. Red, Aubergine oder Ivory Suite sind nach ihrem Farbthema benannt.

Veranda, Innenhof und Dachterrasse laden den Gast ein zum Sonnenbaden, Entspannen und Speisen in ungewöhnlicher Umgebung. Bougainvillea, Palmen, Olivenbäume und Jasmin spenden Schatten und verströmen ihre einzigartigen Düfte.

IN THE MEDINA, the oldest part of Marrakesh, narrow alleys, oriental houses and city palaces dominate while the air is scented with exotic spices. Time seems to stand still. And, here, amidst the hustle and bustle on the streets, stands the Riad Meriem Hotel. This small but very fine house has been lovingly furnished, modelled on Arab culture and art. The New York designer, Thomas Hays, has created a sensual ambience using oriental materials, choice paintings and his own artistic photographs. To preserve authenticity, work on the hotel and its furnishings was undertaken by hand, using only Arab artisans.

Each of the names of the five rooms indicates its given concept: in the Star Suite, for example, glowing stars hang from the ceiling; large Matisse prints decorate the suite of the same name and the Red, Aubergine and Ivory Suites are named after their respective colours.

The veranda, inner courtyard and roof terrace are unusual and pleasant places for the guest to sunbathe, relax and dine. Bougainvillea, palms, olive trees and jasmine provide shade and exude their individual scents.

Address
Riad Meriem
Derb El Cadi 97 – Azbezt
Marrakesh, Medina,
Morocco

Website
www.riadmeriem.com

Ein Bad mit Rosenblüten in sanftem Licht weckt alle Sinne und lädt zu romantischer Zweisamkeit ein. // A rose petal bath with soft lights arouses all the senses and encourages romantic intimacy.

DEUTSCH

ENGLISH

THE RITZ-CARLTON MOSCOW

Moscow, Russia

DIREKT AM WELTBERÜHMTEN Roten Platz, nur wenige Schritte vom Kreml, der Basilius-Kathedrale und dem Lenin-Mausoleum entfernt, bietet das fünfte Ritz-Carlton Hotel in Europa den idealen Standort für Geschäftsreisende und Touristen gleichermaßen. Das elf Etagen hohe Hotelgebäude ist Bestandteil eines »Mixed-use«-Komplexes mit einer Vielzahl an Geschäften und Boutiquen sowie einem Kasino.

Der für das Interieur verantwortliche Designer Peter Silling gestaltete die Innenräume des historischen Gebäudes in klassizistischer Weise. Gleich eine ganze Bandbreite von Marmor in unterschiedlichsten Maserungen und Farben sowie edle Hölzer, Antiquitäten und Werke russischer Künstler gehören zu den von ihm eingesetzten Designelementen. Die Gästezimmer sind mit ebenso klassischen wie eleganten Möbeln ausgestattet. Dunkles, hochglanzpoliertes Kirschholz und Wurzelholzfurniere entfalten eine mondäne Atmosphäre. Die mindestens zehn Quadratmeter großen Badezimmer sind vollständig mit luxuriösem Marmor, separater Dusche und Badewanne, WC-Kabine und Bidet ausgestattet.

STANDING DIRECTLY on the world famous Red Square, only a few steps from the Kremlin, St. Basil's Church and the Lenin Mausoleum, the fifth Ritz-Carlton Hotel in Europe offers the ideal base for both business travellers and tourists. The hotel's eleven floors are part of a mixed-use complex containing a wide range of businesses, boutiques and a casino.

Peter Silling, who was responsible for the interior, used a classic design for the rooms in this historic building. An entire spectrum of marble in a huge variety of markings and colours, costly wood, antiques and the works of Russian artists are all components of his design. The guest rooms are equally fitted with classical and elegant furniture. Dark, highly polished cherrywood and burl wood veneers create a sophisticated atmosphere. The bathrooms, which are over 100 square feet in size are furnished with luxurious marble, separate shower and bathtub, WC cubicle and bidet.

Address
The Ritz-Carlton Moscow
Tverskaya Street 3
Moscow, Russia

Website
www.ritzcarlton.com

In der obersten Etage befindet sich die modern gestaltete Bar mit Terrasse. Die bemerkenswerte Dachkonstruktion aus Glas und Stahl, die Panoramaaussichten auf das lebendige Treiben in der Metropole erlaubt, hat sich schon zu einem Hotspot des Moskauer Nachtlebens etabliert. // A modern style bar with terrace is located on the top floor. The remarkable roof, made of glass and steel, and offering panoramic views of the lively bustle in the city, has already established itself as one of Moscow's hottest night spots.

Die Gästezimmer des The Ritz-Carlton Club, eines »Hotels im Hotel«, befinden sich in den obersten zwei Etagen. Nur mit speziell kodierten Magnetkarten zugänglich, genießen Gäste hier ein besonderes Maß an Sicherheit und privater Atmosphäre. // The rooms at The Ritz-Carlton Club – a »hotel in a hotel«, are on the top two floors. Only accessible with a specially coded magnetic card, guests here can enjoy a greater degree of security and privacy.

DEUTSCH

ENGLISH

SANTA TERESA RESORT

Pantelleria, Italy

PANTELLERIA, eine 83 Quadratkilometer große Vulkaninsel nahe Sizilien, bietet unberührte Natur, herrliche Strände und beeindruckende Landschaften. Mittendrin: das 40 Hektar große Weingut-Hotel Santa Teresa Resort, ein historisches und romantisches Burghotel. Es besteht aus 18 so genannten Dammusi, historischen Bauten, die typisch sind für diese Region und in der Vergangenheit Bauern und Fischern als Bleibe dienten. Renoviert und in einzigartige Herbergen umgewandelt, bieten sie heute ein historisch-rustikales und anspruchsvolles Wohnambiente. Da die ursprüngliche Struktur der Dammusi konserviert wurde, ist jedes Zimmer im romantischen Hotel Santa Teresa anders geschnitten. Darüber hinaus wurde auch bei der Einrichtung Wert auf eine individuelle Gestaltung gelegt. Es kann aus drei Zimmerkategorien gewählt werden: Komfort, Superior und Exzellenz. Diese unterscheiden sich hauptsächlich in ihrer Größe, wobei die Exzellenz-Suiten zudem über einen eigenen Swimmingpool verfügen. Arrangiert sind die Häuser in vier Gruppen, die auf der Anlage des Weinguts verteilt stehen.

PANTELLERIA is a volcanic island near Sicily, covering an area of almost 32 square miles, with unspoilt nature, magnificent beaches and striking landscapes. In the middle of all this is the 100 acre wine estate hotel, the Santa Teresa Resort, a historic and romantic castle hotel. It comprises 18 so-called Dammusi, historical constructions which are typical of the region and served to house peasants and fishermen in the past. Renovated and transformed into unique accommodation, it now offers a rustic, historic and superior living ambience. Since the original structure of the Dammusi has been preserved, each room of the romantic Santa Teresa is different. Furthermore, great store was set by ensuring that each room was individually furnished. One can choose from three room categories – Comfort, Superior and Excellence. The main difference here is size, whereby the Excellence Suites also have their own swimming pool. The houses are arranged in four groups, spread around the wine estate.

Address
Santa Teresa Resort
Via Contrada Monastero
Alto-Sibà
Scauri Siculo, Pantelleria
Sicily, Italy

Website
www.designhotels.com

Die steinernen Mauern der Gebäude fügen sich harmonisch in die natürliche Umgebung der Insel ein: Vulkanischen Ursprungs, ist die Landschaft von Pantelleria geprägt vom schwarzen Boden und bezaubert mit einer gelegentlich eher kargen, aber nicht minder schönen Vegetation. // The stone walls of the buildings blend in perfectly with nature: of volcanic origin, Pantelleria's landscape is characterised by black earth and charms the beholder with its somewhat sparse but nonetheless beautiful vegetation.

Das Resort verfügt über zwei herrliche Swimmingpools, einen Golf-Übungsplatz, einen Fahrradverleih, einen Bootsverleih und vor allem traumhafte Natur. // The resort has two wonderful swimming pools, a golf driving range, bicycle rental, boat rental and, above all, fabulous natural scenery.

DEUTSCH

ENGLISH

SCOTTSDALE MONDRIAN

Scottsdale, USA

DAS MONDRIAN HOTEL, im Herzen der Altstadt Scottsdales gelegen, ist eine originelle Vision moderner Pracht für eine neue Generation mondäner Globetrotter. Inspiriert vom Garten Eden schuf der Designer einen Ort, der für Lebensfreude und Unterhaltung in einer vibrierenden Umgebung steht. Hier sollen Luxus, Genuss und Vergnügen zelebriert werden.

Von der Straße aus sind nur hohe Mauern und die üppigen Gärten des Hotels zu sehen. Durch »Tore«, die über und über mit tropischen Bougainvillea bewachsen sind, geht es für die Gäste über einen weitläufigen, mit Blättern bedruckten roten Teppich in den Eingangsbereich. In der Lobby spendet ein Springbrunnen Kühlung und Kaskaden von weißen Vorhängen bewegen sich in der Luft. Die schamhafte Beschwörung des Paradieses als Thema wird hier erneut aufgenommen: große antike Spiegel, eine geschwungene Bank, an deren Ende ein abstrahierter Affenbrotbaum zur Decke wächst, wolkengleiche Deckenleuchten und eine lebensgroße Abbildung der berühmten Darstellung Dürers von Adam und Eva.

THE MONDRIAN HOTEL, in the heart of old Scottsdale, is an inventive vision of modern glamour for a new generation of sophisticated globetrotters. Inspired by the Garden of Eden, the designer has created a place which presents joie de vivre and entertainment in vibrant surroundings. Luxury, indulgence and pleasure are celebrated here.

From the street, one sees only the high walls and the lush gardens of the hotel. Passing through »gates« fashioned from tropical bougainvillea, the guest walks up a broad red carpet, printed with leaves, to the entrance area. In the lobby, a fountain dispenses a welcome coolness and cascades of white curtains sway in the breeze. The coy evocation of Paradise as a theme is picked up again here with large antique mirrors, a curved bench at one end of which an abstracted baobab tree grows towards the ceiling, cloudlike ceiling lights and a life-size reproduction of Dürer's famous »Adam and Eve«.

Address
Scottsdale Mondrian
7353 East Indian
School Road
Scottsdale, Arizona, USA

Website
www.mondrianscottsdale.com

Im Restaurant Asia de Cuba werden innovative Speisen mit asiatischen und kubanischen Einflüssen serviert. Das Interieur ist fantasievoll, die Oberflächen sind glänzend und prachtvoll. // At the Asia de Cuba restaurant, innovative dishes with Asian and Cuban influences are served. The interior is imaginatively designed, with gorgeous, polished surfaces.

Unzählige Schattierungen von Weiß dominieren nicht nur in der Lobby und den Zimmern, sondern auch im stylischen Restaurant. // Endless shades of white dominate not only in the lobby and rooms, but also in the stylish restaurant.

In der Roten Bar bildet ein riesiger roter Apfel den Mittelpunkt. Üppige scharlachrote Muster und Stoffe kleiden den gesamten Raum. // The focal point in the Red Bar is an enormous red apple. Voluptuous scarlet patterns and textiles adorn the room throughout.

In dekadente schwarze Gaze gehüllt und mit schwarzen Stühlen ausgestattet präsentiert sich die Sky Bar. Das Highlight ist jedoch ein enormes, luxuriöses Bett, das zum Relaxen einlädt. // The Sky Bar is draped in decadent black gauze and furnished with black chairs. The bar's highlight, however, is an enormous, luxurious bed for relaxing.

IN ·
HONO
REM·S
LASII·EP·
Sofà di via Giulia

DEUTSCH

ENGLISH

ST. GEORGE ROMA

Rome, Italy

DAS HARMONISCHE ZUSAMMENSPIEL von Modernem und Historischem sowie die Erschaffung zeitloser Atmosphäre und Eleganz waren die Anforderungen an die Gestaltung dieses Hotels. Ein über 500 Jahre alter Palazzo, ursprünglich von Bramante entworfen, beherbergt das Fünf-Sterne-Haus. Die besondere historische Lage und die Nähe zu zahlreichen Sehenswürdigkeiten, Restaurants und Shoppingmöglichkeiten machen das Hotel zu einem interessanten Ausgangspunkt für eine Stadterkundung. Im Interieur dominiert minimalistisches Design. Inspiriert von Aalto und Jacobsen, schuf der Architekt Lorenzo Bellini ein elegantes, luxuriöses Ambiente. In der Lobby erwarten den Besucher großzügige, komfortable Sitzgelegenheiten in Beige sowie Holzmöbel und -böden und sanftes, indirektes Licht. Die offene Architektur erlaubt Blickbeziehungen zwischen Innen und Außen, Alt und Neu.

Dieses zurückhaltende Farb- und Formenspiel wird in den 64 Zimmern und Suiten, in der Bibliothek, dem Zigarrenzimmer und in der Weinbar konsequent fortgesetzt.

THE HARMONIOUS INTERPLAY of modern and historical and the creation of a timeless atmosphere and elegance were the requirements laid down for the design of this hotel. Originally designed by Bramante, this palazzo which is over 500 years old, now houses this five star hotel. Its particular historic location and its proximity to numerous sights, restaurants and shops makes the hotel an interesting base for discovering the city. Minimalist design dominates inside. Inspired by Aalto and Jacobsen, the architect, Lorenzo Bellini, has created an elegant and luxurious ambience. The lobby, with its soft, indirect lighting, is furnished with roomy and comfortable seats in beige, wooden furniture and wood floors. The open architecture offers views within and outside, of old and of new.

This restrained use of colour and shape is continued consistently in the 64 rooms and suites, the library, the Cigar Room and the wine bar.

Address
St. George Roma
Via Giulia, 62
Rome, Italy

Website
www.stgeorgehotel.it

In der Bibliothek mit dem einladenden Kamin herrscht zeitlose Eleganz. Sanfte Musik im Hintergrund lädt den Gast zum Lesen und Entspannen ein. // In the library with its inviting fireplace, timeless elegance prevails. Soft background music invites the guest to read and relax.

Der exklusive Spa-Bereich setzt auf goldene Akzente, stimmungsvolles Kerzenlicht und dezente, klassische Möblierung. // The exclusive spa area is designed with gold highlights, atmospheric candlelight and discreet, classic furnishings.

DEUTSCH

ENGLISH

SIX SENSES HIDEAWAY YAO NOI

Yao Noi, Thailand

AUF DER INSEL YAO NOI, am Rande eines Naturschutzgebietes, befindet sich dieses außergewöhnliche Resort. Hier werden Luxus, Entspannung und Privatheit großgeschrieben. Dem Gast stehen 56 Villen in fünf Kategorien zur Auswahl, die größte umfasst dabei fast 1.500 Quadratmeter. Sie alle wurden in landestypischer Bauweise und mit traditionellen Materialien gefertigt: Die Wände sind holzgetäfelt und die Dächer wurden mit Palmblättern gedeckt. Im Inneren der Villen wurde viel Wert auf Großzügigkeit und Licht gelegt. Die Badezimmer öffnen sich alle zum Raum hin und erlauben so einen weiten Blick über die Bucht und die atemberaubende Landschaft. Jedes der Gästehäuser besitzt einen eigenen Pool mit direktem Zugang zum Meer. Auf der angrenzenden Terrasse kann der Gast sich entspannen, sonnen und die Ruhe genießen. Für größtmögliche Abgeschiedenheit sorgt das Private In-Villa Dining.

THIS UNUSUAL RESORT is located on the island of Yao Noi at the edge of a nature reserve. Here, luxury, relaxation and privacy are writ large. The guest has a choice of 56 villas in five different categories, with the largest villa covering an area of just over 16,000 square feet. All of the villas have been constructed in the local style using traditional materials: the walls are wood panelled and roofs covered with palm leaves. Inside the villas, great emphasis has been placed on space and light. The bathrooms are open towards all of the rooms, permitting a long view across the bay and the breathtaking landscape. Each of the guest houses has its own pool with direct access to the sea. Guests can relax, sunbathe and enjoy the tranquillity on the adjacent terraces. In-villa dining offers the greatest possible degree of privacy.

Address
Six Senses Hideaway
Yao Noi
56 Moo 5
Yao Noi, Phang-Nga,
Thailand

Website
www.sixsenses.com

Von den Villen hat man einen großartigen Blick auf die spektakulären Felsformationen von Phang Nga. // From the villas one has a fantastic view of the spectacular Phang Nga rock formations.

DEUTSCH

ENGLISH

SIX SENSES HIDEAWAY ZIGHY BAY

Zighy Bay, Oman

DIE KULISSE IST ATEMBERAUBEND: Auf der einen Seite des Six Senses Hideaway im Sultanat Oman liegt eine Bergkette, auf der anderen Seite der 1,6 Kilometer lange Strand der Zighy Bay. 82 Villen mit höchstem Komfort reihen sich an der Bucht. Bei der Ausstattung wurde auf den Einsatz umweltverträglicher Materialien Wert gelegt. Das Resort besticht durch seinen ganz besonderen Stil: Moderne Architektur verbindet sich mit traditionellen omanischen Stilelementen. Die Steinhäuser öffnen sich zum Meer hin und lassen den Blick auf die Bucht frei. Typische Holzmöbel, hell getünchte Wände sowie Stoffe in Beige und Orange lassen das Innere der Villen warm und elegant erscheinen.

Zu den Annehmlichkeiten des Hotels gehören Restaurants, Bars, ein Weinkeller sowie eine ganz besondere Art des Speisens: »Dining on the Edge« – auf den umgebenden Bergen lädt eine Lounge zu entspanntem Essen und Genießen ein, einzigartiger Blick inklusive.

THE BACKDROP IS BREATHTAKING: on one side of the Six Senses Hideaway in the Sultanate of Oman there is a mountain chain while on the other, one has the Zighy Bay beach, almost a mile long. 82 extremely comfortable villas line the bay. They have been furnished with a keen eye on environmentally friendly materials. The resort's particular charm lies in its very special style: modern architecture fuses with traditional Omani style elements. The stone houses are open to the sea, giving a free view of the bay. Typical wooden furniture, whitewashed walls and textiles in beige and orange give the interiors a warm and elegant appearance.

The hotel's amenities include restaurants, bars, a wine cellar and a most unusual concept – »Dining on the Edge«: a lounge built on the surrounding mountains invites guests to enjoy a relaxed meal and enjoy the unique view at the same time.

Address
Six Senses Hideaway Zighy Bay
Zighy Bay, Musandam Peninsula, Oman

Website
www.sixsenses.com

Kleine Details, wie etwa in die Steinwände eingelassene Sitzmöglichkeiten, zeigen den besonderen Charme des Resorts. // Small details, such as the seating recessed into the stone walls illustrate the resort's particular charm.

Nachts werden die Häuser und der Pool dramatisch beleuchtet und bilden so eine fantastische Kulisse für romantische Dinner oder einen abendlichen Spaziergang am Strand. // At night, the houses and pool are dramatically illuminated, providing a fantastic backdrop for romantic dinners or a nocturnal stroll on the beach.

DEUTSCH

ENGLISH

SIXTY HOTEL

Riccione, Italy

DIE ADRIAKÜSTE zwischen Rimini und Ravenna ist zweifellos das Mekka der italienischen Szenegänger. Seit Jahren ist sie Treffpunkt für ein extravagantes, wildes Nachtleben. Und nun hat hier auch ein außergewöhnliches Hotel seine Pforten geöffnet: das Sixty Hotel. Namensgeber ist das gleichnamige Kultlabel, dessen Jeans schon lange heiß begehrte Lieblingsstücke junger Fashion Victims sind. Konzipiert für ein junges, wildes und hippes Publikum, das fernab vom Gewöhnlichen Urlaub machen will, repräsentiert das Haus eine gelungene Mischung aus Retro-Chic, Moderne und Kunst. Schon äußerlich hebt es sich von seiner Umgebung ab. Eine Hülle mit organischen Öffnungen im Retro-Stil umschließt das ursprüngliche Gebäude aus den Fünfzigerjahren. Nachts mit blauen Neonröhren beleuchtet, ist es weithin sichtbar.

Im Inneren konnten sich 30 junge Künstler in den Zimmern kreativ austoben und so individuelle Unterkünfte schaffen. Die Räume erstrahlen in grellen Farben, mit Graffiti oder ausgefallenen Sprüchen an den Wänden.

THE ADRIATIC COAST between Rimini and Ravenna is without doubt a mecca for the Italian in crowd. For years it has been the venue for extravagant and wild nightlife. Now, the flamboyant Sixty Hotel has opened its doors there. It is called after the cult label of the same name, whose jeans have long been a favourite with young fashion victims. Designed for a young, wild and hip public, which wants a holiday with a difference, this hotel is a successful mix of retro chic, modernity and art. From the outside, the hotel already sets itself apart from its surroundings. The building, erected in the 1950s, is encased in retro style with organic openings. Lit by blue neon tubes at night, it is visible far and wide.

Inside, 30 young artists were given a free hand in the rooms, creating individual accommodations. They dazzle in garish colours, with graffiti or eccentric slogans on the walls.

Address
Sixty Hotel
Via Milano 54
Riccione, Italy

Website
www.sixtyhotel.com

Schon in der Eingangshalle wird das innovative Konzept des Hotels deutlich: Moderne Kunstwerke und knallige Farben werden mit Designklassikern, wie etwa dem Tulip Chair von Eero Saarinen, kombiniert. // The hotel's innovative concept becomes clear immediately one steps into the entrance area: modern art works and vibrant colours are combined with design classics, such as Eero Saarinen's Tulip Chair.

Die Gestaltung der äußeren Hülle erinnert an Cartoon- und Comiczeichnungen und lässt ungewöhnliche Ein- und Ausblicke zu. // The outer shell is reminiscent of cartoons and comic drawings and affords an unusually great number of insights and views.

»Someone was killed in this room« und »Don't fall asleep« – warnt der Künstler Nicola Gobbetto den Gast. // »Someone was killed in this room« and »Don't fall asleep« are the warnings to guests given by artist Nicola Gobbetto.

DEUTSCH

ENGLISH

SOFITEL METROPOLE HANOI

Hanoi, Vietnam

DAS SOFITEL HANOI HOTEL wurde im französischen Kolonialstil im Jahr 1901 erbaut. Es ist ein Haus mit einer bewegten Geschichte: Botschafter, Schriftsteller, Staatsoberhäupter und Unternehmer haben bisher zu seinen Gästen gezählt.

Bei der heutigen Gestaltung ist das Hotel seinen Ursprüngen treu geblieben: In der Lobby hängen unter dem sorgfältig renovierten Glasdach antike Ventilatoren, die die flirrende Hitze Vietnams vertreiben sollen.

Dem Gast werden in den 363 Zimmern und Suiten modernster Komfort und technisches Equipment, wie Breitband-Internet, LCD- und DVD-Spieler, geboten. Im Metropol-Flügel ist noch der Charme des kolonialen Zeitalters spürbar: Dunkles Holz, prächtige Stoffe und Teppiche zeichnen die historischen Zimmer aus. Im zweiten, dem Opera-Flügel, setzt man auf zeitgemäße Innenraumgestaltung in neoklassischer Eleganz. Hier sind die vorherrschenden Farben Schwarz und Weiß, mit roten Farbtupfern oder modern interpretierten floralen Tapetenmustern. Zum Hotel gehören auch ein schöner Innengarten sowie Restaurants mit ausgezeichneter französischer Cuisine und Spezialitäten aus Hanoi.

THE SOFITEL HANOI HOTEL was built in the French colonial style in 1901 and has had a turbulent 100-year history: ambassadors, writers, heads of state and entrepreneurs have numbered amongst the guests.

Today's design remains faithful to the building's origins: in the lobby, hanging beneath the carefully renovated glass roof, are antique fans, which strive to dispel Vietnam's daze-inducing heat.

In the 363 rooms and suites, the guest is provided with up to the minute comfort and technical equipment such as broadband internet, LCD and DVD players. In the Metropole Wing, the charm of the colonial era is still apparent: dark wood, together with sumptuous textiles and carpets make these historic rooms stand out. In the Opera Wing, the hotel has gone for contemporary interior design with neoclassical elegance. Here, the dominant colours are black and white with daubs of red or floral patterned wallpaper with a modern spin. The hotel also has a pretty inner courtyard and restaurants offering excellent French cuisine and Hanoi specialities.

Address
Sofitel Metropole Hanoi
15 Ngo Quyen Street
Hanoi, Vietnam

Website
www.sofitel.com

Das Hotel erhebt Genuss und Gastlichkeit zur Lebenskunst. Die verschiedenen Bars und Restaurants sind Orte der Geselligkeit, die die Tradition der französischen Kochkunst mit den neuesten Trends der internationalen Küche verbinden. //
The hotel raises indulgence and hospitality to new levels. The various bars and restaurants are convivial and combine the traditional French art of cooking with the latest trends in international cuisine.

EVA AIR
星際娛樂場

DEUTSCH

ENGLISH

STARWORLD HOTEL MACAU

Macau

DIESES 38-GESCHOSSIGE HOTEL mit Kasino steht im Herzen des Spiel- und Vergnügungsviertels Macaus. Das Gebäude besitzt eine zweite Haut aus Glas, in die LEDs eingebaut sind und die mit den verschiedensten Farben und Mustern beleuchtet werden kann. So erstrahlt das Hotel weithin sichtbar und wird zu einem Wahrzeichen der glitzernden Avenida da Amizade. Im Inneren beherrschen luxuriöse Materialien, glamouröse Accessoires und kräftige Farben die Einrichtung. Neun verschiedene Restaurants und Bars, ein Pool und Spa-Bereich im 17. Geschoss sowie eine Vielzahl an Vergnügungs- und Freizeiteinrichtungen lassen keine Wünsche offen.

Die 500 Zimmer und Suiten sind alle mit dem höchsten Komfort und modernster technischer Ausstattung versehen. Großzügige Badezimmer mit raumhohen Glaswänden vermitteln dem Gast ein Gefühl von Weite und bieten einzigartige Ausblicke in die aufregende Umgebung oder den Nachthimmel.

THIS 38-STOREY HOTEL with casino is in the heart of Macau's gaming and pleasure district. The building has a second skin, made of glass, in which LEDs have been installed, so that it can be illuminated with a huge variety of colours and patterns. Thus the hotel's brilliance can be seen far and wide, making it into the landmark of the glittering Avenida da Amizade. Inside, luxurious materials, glamorous accessories and vibrant colours define the interior design. Nine different restaurants and bars, a pool and spa area on the 17th floor and a wide range of leisure and recreational facilities leave nothing to be desired.

The 500 rooms and suites are all extremely comfortable and fitted with the latest technical equipment. The spacious bathrooms with their glass walls give the guest a sense of space and ensure that he has unparalleled views of the exciting surroundings and the night sky.

Address
StarWorld Hotel
Avenida da Amizade,
Macau

Website
www.starworldmacau.com

In den Zimmern verschmilzt asiatische Handwerkskunst mit modernem Design zu einem außergewöhnlichen Ambiente. // In the rooms, Asian handicraft fuses with modern design to create an extraordinary ambience.

Die Präsidentensuite allein verfügt über mehr als 500 Quadratmeter Fläche. Marmorböden und goldglänzende Wände verweisen bereits im Eingangsbereich auf das luxuriöse Interieur, das den Gast hier erwartet. // The Presidential Suite alone has an area of over 5,300 square feet. Marble floors and gold glittering walls in the entrance area are a pointer to the luxurious ambience which awaits the guest inside.

POST TELEFON
Vene

DEUTSCH

ENGLISH

HOTEL TELEGRAAF

Tallinn, Estonia

DER NAME DIESE HOTELS kommt nicht von ungefähr. Das im 19. Jahrhundert erbaute Gebäude in der Innenstadt von Tallinn beherbergte früher eine Telegrafenstation. Von hier aus gingen während der sowjetischen Ära die entscheidenden Meldungen durch den Eisernen Vorhang. Nun wurde das elegante Stadthaus saniert und zu einem nicht minder eleganten Hotel umgebaut. Hier wird die geheimnisvolle Atmosphäre eines vergangenen Jahrhunderts zelebriert.

Wände in dunklen und kräftigen Farben, schwere Stoffe, prächtige Teppiche, prunkvolle Kronleuchter und klassisches Mobiliar lassen eine längst vergangene Zeit wiederaufleben.

THIS HOTEL'S NAME isn't merely a coincidence. The building, erected in the 19th century in Tallinn's inner city, once housed a telegraph station. During the Soviet era, it was from here that many crucial messages passed through the Iron Curtain. Now this elegant townhouse has been restored and converted into a no less elegant hotel. Here, the secretive atmosphere of the past century is celebrated.

Walls in dark and vibrant colours, voluptuous textiles, gorgeous carpets, magnificent chandeliers and classic furniture recreate the atmosphere of distant times.

Address
Hotel Telegraaf
Vene 9
Tallinn, Estonia

Website
www.telegraafhotel.com

Im Restaurant speist man unter schweren Lüstern und den wachsamen Augen ehemaliger Berühmtheiten. // In the restaurant one dines beneath pendulous chandeliers and the watchful eyes of former famous personages.

Romantische Zweisamkeit mit Ausblicken auf die aufstrebende estnische Hauptstadt kann im Badezimmer der Suiten genossen werden. // In the suite bathrooms, one can enjoy romantic intimacy and views of the emerging Estonian capital.

Ein historischer Telefonapparat – solche liebevoll ausgewählten Details machen den Charme dieses besonderen Hotels aus. // An old telephone – it is this eye to detail which gives this special hotel its charm.

DEUTSCH

ENGLISH

VEDEMA RESORT SANTORINI

Megalohori, Greece

DIESES RESORT, auf einer der wohl schönsten griechischen Inseln, Santorini, gelegen, entführt seine Gäste in eine Welt voller Anmut und Mythen.

Die 45 großzügig bemessenen Villen sind, wie eine kleine Stadt, von einer Mauer umschlossen und stehen inmitten eines Weinguts aus dem 15. Jahrhundert. Die Einrichtung verbindet traditionelle griechische Architektur mit modernen Elementen und strahlenden Farben. Alle Häuser bieten Bäder aus Marmor, Möbel in inseltypischem Design und eine private Terrasse. Die zehn Pool-Villen bestechen durch ihre erfrischende, minimalistische Ausstattung, inspiriert durch die einfache Architektur der Insel-Hütten. Das Highlight ist jedoch die Präsidenten-Suite. 175 Quadratmeter, drei luxuriös ausgestattete Zimmer, neueste Unterhaltungselektronik, eine Terrasse mit integriertem Whirlpool und der exklusive Privat-Pool ermöglichen dem Gast ein Erlebnis der besonderen Art.

THIS RESORT on Santorini, which must be one of the loveliest Greek islands, entices its guests into a world full of beauty and myth.

The 45 generously sized villas are enclosed, city-like, by walls, and stand in the middle of a 15th century wine growing estate. The interior design combines traditional Greek architecture with modern elements and dazzling colours. All of the villas have marble-clad bathrooms, furniture in the local style and a private terrace. The refreshing, minimalist furnishings of the ten pool villas, inspired by the simple architecture of the island huts, is most attractive. The highlight however is the Presidential Suite. With an area of over 1,800 square feet, three luxuriously appointed rooms, the latest entertainment technology, a terrace with integrated whirlpool and an exclusive private pool, the guest can be sure of an incomparable stay.

Address
Vedema Resort Santorini
Megalohori
Santorini, Greece

Website
www.vedema.gr

Weiß und Türkis – die typischen Farben der Insel – dominieren die exquisite Einrichtung der Präsidenten-Suite. Hier kann der Gast sich an seinem privaten Pool sonnen, entspannen oder ein intimes Dinner genießen. // White and turquoise, the typical colours of the island, dominate in the exquisite furnishing of the Presidential Suite. Here the guest can sunbathe, relax or enjoy an intimate dinner beside the private pool.

In den Appartements und Suiten beherrschen kräftige Blau-, Pink- und Gelbtöne die Einrichtung. // Vibrant blue, pink and yellow are the main colours in the apartments.

Die abendliche, stimmungsvolle Beleuchtung leitet den Gast zu den verschiedenen Restaurants und Bars. // The dusky, atmospheric lighting guides the guests to the various restaurants and bars.

DEUTSCH

ENGLISH

HOTEL WASSERTURM

Hamburg, Germany

DER EHEMALIGE WASSERTURM im Sternschanzepark wurde in den vergangenen zweieinhalb Jahren aufwendig umgebaut und saniert und beherbergt nun ein Vier-Sterne-Plus-Hotel. Vom Eingang in der Straße Sternschanze gelangen die Hotelgäste über ein 25 Meter langes Rollband in einem Tunnel zur Rezeption und Lobby des 60 Meter hohen, denkmalgeschützten Gebäudes. Dort zeigt sich dem Gast ein spannendes Zusammenspiel aus zeitgemäßem Design und dem historischen Kreuzgewölbe des alten Wasserturms.

226 Zimmer sind auf 17 Etagen verteilt, darunter acht Junior-Suiten und zwei Turm-Suiten, die einen faszinierenden Blick über die Stadt offerieren. Alle Zimmer sind in dezenten Weiß-, Beige- und Brauntönen gehalten und beeindrucken durch ihr klares, minimalistisches Design.

THE FORMER WATER TOWER in Sternschanzepark has been completely restored and converted over the last two years and now houses a four star plus hotel. At the entrance on Sternschanze Strasse, the guest steps onto a conveyor belt, 82 feet long, passing through a tunnel to the reception and lobby of this listed building, which is nearly 200 feet high. There the guest can enjoy the exciting interplay between contemporary design and the historic cross-vault of the old water tower.

The 226 rooms, including eight Junior Suites and two Tower Suites are divided over 17 floors, offering a fascinating view of the city. All of the rooms are decorated in restrained shades of white, beige and brown and are pleasingly clean and minimalist in design.

Address
Hotel Wasserturm
Sternschanze 6
Hamburg, Germany

Website
www.moevenpick-hotels.com

An mehreren Orten im Hotel weckt die Installation Memory der Künstlerin Ulrike Böhme in den Gästen Reminiszenzen an die einstige Atmosphäre im Wasserturm. Diese »Erinnerungsmodule« sind überall im Haus zu entdecken: Im Erschließungstunnel werfen imaginäre Wasserflächen Lichtreflexionen an Wände und Decken. Wassergeräusche und ein fernes Nebelhorn verdichten zusätzlich die atmosphärische Installation. // In several places throughout the hotel, the installation Memory by the artist, Ulrike Böhme, lead the guest to reminisce on the water tower's earlier atmosphere. These »memory modules« are to be found all over the hotel: in the excavation tunnel, imaginary water surfaces reflect light onto walls and ceiling. The sound of water and a distant foghorn further enhance the feel of this atmospheric installation.

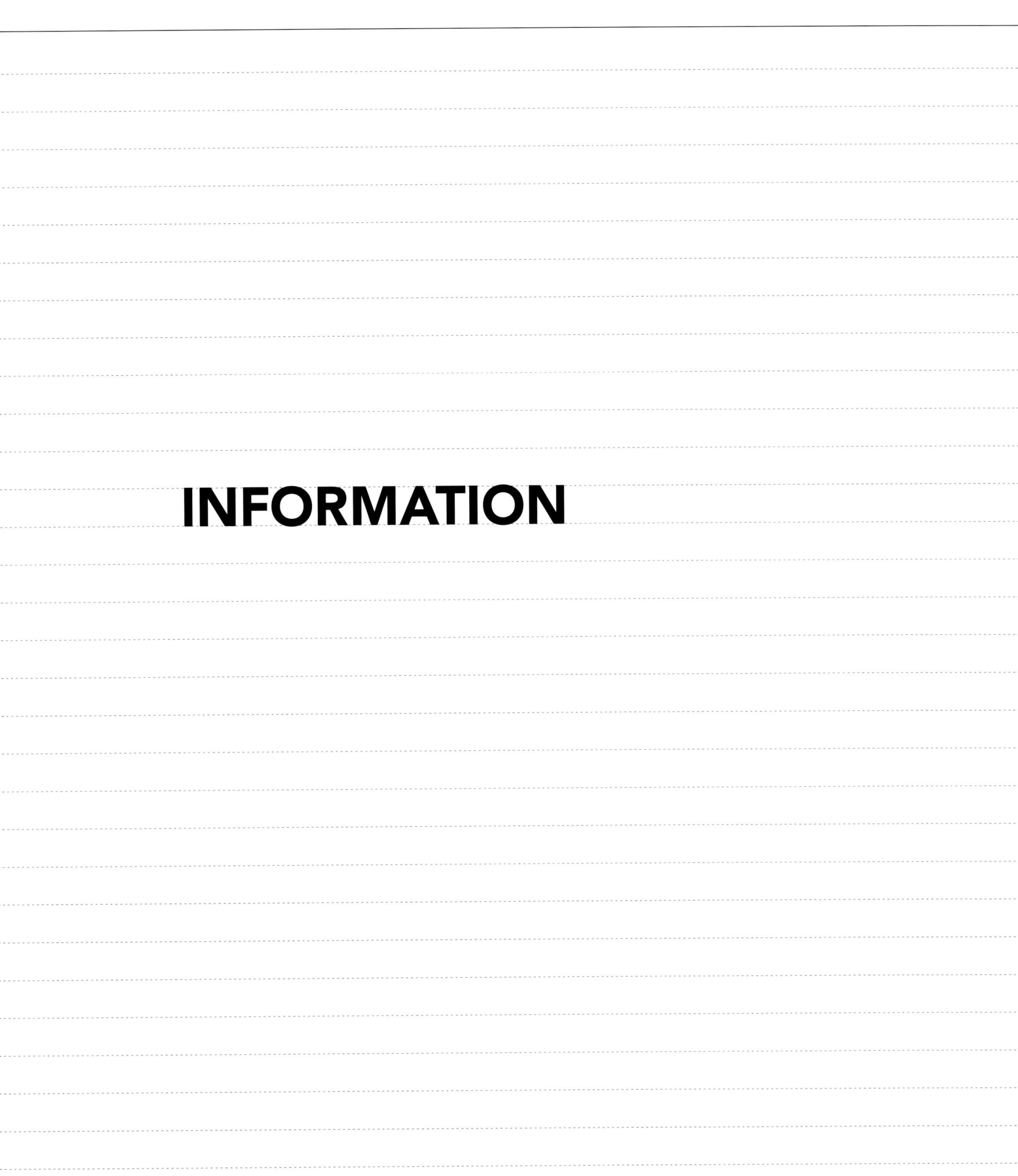

INFORMATION

ADAM & EVE HOTEL
Iskele Mevkii
Antalya, Turkey
www.adamevehotels.com
Eren Talu
Photos: © courtesy by Adam & Eve

HOTEL ANDAZ
40 Liverpool Street
London, UK
london.liverpoolstreet.andaz.com
Photos: © courtesy by Hyatt Group

AIRPORT HOTEL
Flughafenstrasse 50
Stuttgart, Germany
www.moevenpick-hotels.com
Matteo Thun & Partners
Photos: © courtesy by
Mövenpick Hotels

AVALON HOTEL
Kungstorget 9
Gothenburg, Sweden
www.avalonhotel.se
Semrén & Månsson Arkitektkontor
www.semren-mansson.se
Photos: © courtesy by Avalon Hotels

ALTSTADT VIENNA
Kirchengasse 41
Vienna, Austria
www.altstadt.at
Matteo Thun & Partners
Photos: © courtesy by
Altstadt Vienna

BLUE PALACE RESORT & SPA
Plaka, Elounda
Crete, Greece
www.bluepalace.gr
3SK Stylianidis Architects
www.3sk.gr
Photos: © George Lizardo s.

CASA COLOMBO
231 Galle Road
Colombo, Sri Lanka
www.casacolombo.com
Lalin Jinasena
Photos: © courtesy by
Casa Colombo

CERÊS AM MEER
Strandpromenade 24
Baltic Resort of Binz,
Rügen, Germany
www.ceres-hotel.de
Moritz Lau-Engehausen
Photos: © Klaus Stemmler

THE CHARLES HOTEL
Sophienstrasse 28
Munich, Germany
www.charleshotel.de
Hilmer, Sattler & Albrecht
www.h-s-a.de
Photos: © Bernd Ducker

THE CHEDI MILAN
Via Villapizzone 24
Milan, Italy
www.thechedimilan.com
Jaya Ibrahim, Jaya Associates
Photos: © Courtesy by Bulgari PR

COCO PALM BODU HITHI
North Male Atoll, Maldives
www.cocopalm.com
Photos: © courtesy by
Coco Collection

CHISWICK MORAN HOTEL
626 Chiswick High Road
London, UK
www.chiswickhotellondon.co.uk
Project Orange
www.projectorange.com
Photos: © Gareth Gardner

CUBE BIBERWIER-LERMOOS
Fernpass-Strasse 71-72
Biberwier-Lermoos, Austria
www.cube-biberwier.at
Photos: © courtesy by CUBE

THE ETON HOTEL
535 Pudong Avenue
Shanghai, China
www.theetonhotel.com
Photos: © courtesy by Worldhotels

EVASON ANA MANDARA VILLAS & SIX SENSES SPA
Le Lai Street, Ward 5
Dalat, Vietnam
www.sixsenses.com
Photos: © courtesy by Six Senses

EYNSHAM HALL
North Leigh, Witney
Oxfordshire, UK
www.eynshamhall.com
Berman Guedes Stretton
www.bgsarchitects.co.uk
Photos: © courtesy by BGS
Architects Ltd

FÄHRHAUS HOTEL
Heefwai 1
Sylt-Ost/Munkmarsch, Germany
www.faehrhaus-sylt.de
Photos: © Hassel/WeberBenAmmar PR

FALCONARA CHARMING HOUSE & RESORT
Località Falconara
Butera, Sicily, Italy
www.designhotels.com
Antonio Vitale ñ B. Castrense,
Roberto e Antonella,
Chiaramonte Bordonaro
Photos: © courtesy by designhotels

THE FORTRESS
Koggala Beach
Galle, Sri Lanka
www.thefortress.lk
Photos: © courtesy by Per Aquum

FARNHAM ESTATE HOTEL
Farnham Estate
Cavan, Irland
www.farnhamestate.ie
Project Orange
www.projectorange.com
Photos: © courtesy by Radisson SAS
Hotels, Gareth Gardner

FIRST HOTEL GRIMS GRENKA
Kongens gate 5
Oslo, Norway
www.firsthotels.com
Kristin Jarmund Architects
www.kjark.no
Photos: © courtesy by designhotels

GERBERMÜHLE
Gerbermühlstrasse 105
Frankfurt am Main, Germany
www.gerbermuehle.de
Jochem Jourdan,
Jourdan & Müller PAS
www.jourdan-mueller.de
Oana Rosen
Photos: © courtesy by designhotels

GOLDMAN 25HOURS
Hanauer Landstrasse 127
Frankfurt am Main, Germany
www.25hours-hotels.com
Photos: © courtesy by 25hours

GRAMERCY PARK HOTEL
2 Lexington Avenue
New York City, USA
www.gramercyparkhotel.com
Julian Schnabel
Photos: © courtesy by
Ian Schrager Group

GRAND HOTEL CENTRAL
Via Layetana, 30
Barcelona, Spain
www.grandhotelcentral.com
Oriol Tintoré, TMA Arquitectura
www.tmaarquitectura.net
Sandra Tarruella & Isabel Lopéz
www.tarruellalopez.com
Photos: © MWPR

HOSPES VILLA PAULITA
Av. Pons i Gasch, 15
Puigcerdà, Spain
www.hospes.es
Photos: © courtesy by Hospes

HYATT REGENCY HAKONE RESORT & SPA
1320 Gora Hakone-machi,
Ashigarashimo-gun
Hakone, Kanagawa Prefecture, Japan
hakone.regency.hyatt.com
Photos: © courtesy by Hyatt Group

HOTEL DE ROME
Behrenstrasse 37
Berlin, Germany
www.hotelderome.com
Tommaso Ziffer
www.tommasoziffer.it
Photos: © Giorgio Baroni

HAYMARKET HOTEL
1 Suffolk Place
London, UK
www.firmdale.com
Kit Kemp
Photos: © courtesy by
Haymarket Hotel

J.K. PLACE
Via Prov. Marina Grande
Capri, Italy
www.jkplace.com
Michael Bonan
Photos: © courtesy by J.K.Place

JETWING VIL UYANA
Sigiriya, Sri Lanka
www.viluyana.com
Photos: © courtesy by
Jetwing Hotels Ltd

HOTEL KAPOK
No. 16 Donghuamen Street
Beijing, China
www.hotelkapok.com
Photos: © Shu He

KEATING HOTEL
432 F st
San Diego, USA
www.thekeating.com
Paolo Pininfarina/Pininfarina S.p.a.
extra.pininfarina.com
Photos: © John Edward Linden

LA PURIFICADORA
Callejón de la
10 Norte 802,
Paseo San Francisco
Puebla, Mexico
www.lapurificadora.com
Legorreta + Legorreta, Mexico
www.legorretalegorreta.com
Serrano Monjaraz Arquitectos
www.serranomonjaraz.com
Photos: © courtesy by designhotels

LA RÉSERVE
10 Place du Trocadéro
Paris, France
www.lareserve-paris.com
Rémi Tessier
www.remi-tessier.com
Photos: © courtesy by designhotels

LABRIZ SILHOUETTE
Silhouette Island,
Seychelles
www.labriz-seychelles.com
Photos: © Shoumo Mukherjee

LÁNCHÍD 19
Lánchíd utca 19-21
Budapest, Hungary
www.lanchid19hotel.hu
Radius B+S Ltd. & KB Design,
Péter Sugár, László Benczúr,
László Kara
Photos: © courtesy by
designhotels

LOVE HOTEL
Concept
Studio 63 Architecture + Design
www.studio63.it
Photos: © courtesy by Studio 63

MARQUÉS DE RISCAL
Calle Torrea, 1
Elciego, Spain
www.starwoodhotels.com
Frank O. Gehry
www.foga.com
Photos: © courtesy by Thomas
Mayer Archive

MÖVENPICK RESORT & SPA
Allee des Cocotiers
Bel Ombre, Mauritius
www.moevenpick-hotels.com
Photos: © courtesy by
Mövenpick Hotels

MILLENNIUM HILTON BANGKOK
123 Charoennakorn Road
Bangkok, Thailand
www.hilton.com
Photos: © courtesy by Hilton Group

ONE WORLD HOTEL
First Avenue
Petaling Jaya, Selangor
Malaysia
www.oneworldhotel.com.my
Photos: © courtesy by Worldhotels

MOHR LIFE RESORT
Innsbruckerstrasse 40
Lermoos, Austria
www.mohr-life-resort.at
Photos: © Mario Jack Coble

THE POD HOTEL
230 East 51st St
New York City, USA
www.thepodhotel.com
Vanessa Guilford
Photos: © courtesy by The Pod Hotel

HOTEL PORTO PALÁCIO
Av. Boavista, 1269
Porto, Portugal
www.hotelportopalacio.com
plajer & franz studio
www.plajer-franz.de
Photos: © courtesy by
plajer & franz studio

PARK HOTEL MUMBAI
No 1, Sector 10, CBD Belapur
Navi Mumbai, India
navimumbai.theparkhotels.com
Photos: © courtesy by
The Park Hotels

RADISSON HOTEL PUDONG CENTURY PARK
Ying Chun Road
Pudong, Shanghai, China
www.radisson.com
Photos: © courtesy by Radisson
Hotels & Resorts

RIAD MERIEM
Derb El Cadi 97 – Azbezt
Marrakesh, Medina,
Morocco
www.riadmeriem.com
Thomas Hays Interiors
www.thomashaysinteriors.com
Photos: © courtesy by Thomas Hays Interiors

THE RITZ-CARLTON MOSCOW
Tverskaya Street 3
Moscow, Russia
www.ritzcarlton.com
Peter Silling
Photos: © courtesy by Ritz-Carlton, vision-photos.de

SANTA TERESA RESORT
Via Contrada Monastero Alto-Sibà
Scauri Siculo, Pantelleria
Sicily, Italy
www.designhotels.com
Photos: © courtesy by designhotels

SCOTTSDALE MONDRIAN
7353 East Indian
School Road
Scottsdale, Arizona, USA
www.mondrianscottsdale.com
Benjamin Noriega-Ortiz
www.bnodesign.com
Photos: © courtesy by Morgans Hotel Group

ST. GEORGE ROMA
Via Giulia, 62
Rome, Italy
www.stgeorgehotel.it
Lorenzo Bellini
www.lorenzobellini.com

SIX SENSES HIDEAWAY YAO NOI
56 Moo 5
Yao Noi, Phang-Nga, Thailand
www.sixsenses.com
Photos: © courtesy by Six Senses

SIX SENSES HIDEAWAY ZIGHY BAY
Zighy Bay,
Musandam Peninsula, Oman
www.sixsenses.com
Photos: © courtesy by Six Senses

SIXTY HOTEL
Via Milano 54
Riccione, Italy
www.sixtyhotel.com
Studio 63 Architecture + Design
www.studio63.it
Photos: © Yael Pincus

SOFITEL METROPOLE HANOI
15 Ngo Quyen Street
Hanoi, Vietnam
www.sofitel.com
Photos: © courtesy by Sofitel Luxury Hotels

STARWORLD HOTEL
Avenida da Amizade, Macau
www.starworldmacau.com
Rocco Design
www.roccodesign.com.hk
Photos: © courtesy by Worldhotels

HOTEL TELEGRAAF
Vene 9
Talinn, Estonia
www.telegraafhotel.com
Photos: © courtesy by Small Luxury Hotels of the World Limited

VEDEMA RESORT SANTORINI
Megalohori
Santorini, Greece
www.vedema.gr
Photos: © courtesy by Starwood Hotels

HOTEL WASSERTURM
Sternschanze 6
Hamburg, Germany
www.moevenpick-hotels.com
Falk von Tettenborn
www.tettenborn.net
Cornelia Markus-Diedenhofen
Photos: © courtesy by Mövenpick Hotels, Aloys Kiefer

And all product photos:
Fabian Hammans

IMPRINT

Die Deutsche Bibliothek verzeichnet diese Publikation in der Deutschen Nationalbibliografie; detaillierte bibliografische Daten sind im Internet über http://dnb.ddb.de abrufbar.

ISBN 978-3-938666-47-0

Autor:	Joachim Fischer
Redaktion:	Sabine Marinescu, Joachim Fischer
Gestaltung:	Fabian Hammans
Lektorat:	Bettina Groß, Uta Keil
Übersetzung:	FRONT RUNNER Corporate Communication
Produktion:	klett / fischer [architecture- and design-publishing] www.klett-fischer.com

Sämtliche Angaben in diesem Band wurden durch die Redaktion nach bestem Wissen und Gewissen zusammengestellt. Sie basieren ausschließlich auf den dem Verlag zur Verfügung gestellten und freigezeichneten Informationen der Architekturbüros bzw. Hotels. Der Verlag übernimmt keine Haftung für Richtigkeit und Vollständigkeit sowie urheberrechtliche Unstimmigkeiten und verweist auf die genannten Quellen (Architekturbüros/Hotels).